THE

𝔚𝔦𝔱𝔠𝔥𝔠𝔯𝔞𝔣𝔱 𝔇𝔢𝔩𝔲𝔰𝔦𝔬𝔫

IN

NEW ENGLAND:

ITS

RISE, PROGRESS, AND TERMINATION,

AS EXHIBITED BY

DR. COTTON MATHER,

IN

THE WONDERS OF THE INVISIBLE WORLD;

AND BY

MR. ROBERT CALEF,

IN HIS

MORE WONDERS OF THE INVISIBLE WORLD.

WITH A

Preface, Introduction, and Notes,

BY SAMUEL G. DRAKE.

IN THREE VOLUMES.

VOL. III.

More Wonders of the Invisible World.

British Library Cataloguing-in-Publication Data
A catalogue record for this book is available from
the British Library

The Folklore and History of Witchcraft

Witchcraft, also called 'witchery' or 'spellcraft' is the use of magical faculties, most commonly for religious, divinatory or medicinal purposes. The belief and the practice of magic has been present since the earliest human cultures and continues to have an important religious and medicinal role in many cultures today. The concept of witchcraft and sorcery, and those accused of its practice have sadly often been utilised as a scapegoat for human misfortune. This was particularly the case in the early modern period of Europe where witchcraft came to be seen as part of a vast diabolical conspiracy of individuals in league with the Devil undermining Christianity. This eventually led to large-scale witch hunts, especially in Protestant Europe. Witch hunts continue to this day with tragic consequences.

Witches and witchcraft have long been objects of fear, and occasionally admiration in traditional folkloric tales. The Ancient Greeks believed in a deity named 'Hecate' who was said to be the god of all witches, as well as hexes, poisonous plants and sorcery. One of the other names she was known by, 'Chthonia' literally translates as 'of the underworld.' Such folkloric beliefs inspired the character of 'Circe' in Homer's *Odyssey*. Here, Circe lived on an island named Aeaea, where she turned passing sailors into wolves and lions. Odysseus only narrowly escaped transformation due to a magical plant. Indian folkloric tradition has an all-together darker tale, that of 'Chedipe'; a woman who died during childbirth. She was said to ride on a tiger at night-fall, and enter people's houses. Then without waking a soul, she would suck the life out of each man through the toes. The most famous English portrayal of witchcraft is the three witches in Shakespeare's Macbeth, inspired by the tale of the Moirai. These three sisters—or fates—are the first characters the audience encounters and act as agents of destruction, sending Macbeth into a spiral of corruption and obsession.

In Early Modern European tradition witches were stereotypically, though not exclusively women. European pagan belief in witchcraft was associated with the goddess Diana, and was fully believed by much of the population. With the advent of Christianity however, such beliefs were dismissed as 'diabolical fantasies' by medieval Christian authors. Early converts to Christianity looked to Christian clergy to work magic more effectively than the old methods under Roman paganism, and Christianity provided a methodology involving saints and relics, similar to the gods and amulets of the Pagan world. The Protestant Christian explanation for witchcraft, such as those typified in the confessions of the Pendle witches (a series of famous witch trials which took place in Lancashire in 1612), commonly involves a diabolical pact or at least an appeal to the intervention of the spirits of evil.

The witches or wizards engaged in such practices were alleged to reject Jesus and the sacraments; observe 'the witches' sabbath' (performing infernal rites that often parodied the Mass or other sacraments of the Church); pay

Divine honour to the Prince of Darkness; and, in return, receive from him preternatural powers. It was a folkloric belief that a Devil's Mark, like the brand on cattle, was placed upon a witch's skin by the devil to signify that this pact had been made. The Church and European society were not always so zealous in hunting witches or blaming them for misfortunes. Saint Boniface declared in the eighth century that belief in the existence of witches was un-Christian. The emperor Charlemagne further decreed that the burning of supposed witches was a pagan custom that would be punished by the death penalty. In 820 the Bishop of Lyon repudiated the belief that witches could make bad weather, fly in the night and change their shape. This denial was accepted into Canon Law until it was reversed in later centuries as witch hunts gained force.

It should be noted, that not all witches were assumed to be harmful practitioners of their craft. In England the provision of curative magic was the job of a witch doctor, also known as a cunning man, white witch, or wise man. The term 'witch doctor' was in use in England before it came to be associated with Africa. 'Toad Doctors' were also credited with the ability to undo evil witchcraft. Since the twentieth century, witchcraft has become a designated branch of modern paganism. It is most notably practiced in the Wiccan and witchcraft traditions, which are generally portrayed as revivals of pre-Christian European ritual and spirituality. They are understood to involve varying degrees of magic, shamanism, folk medicine, spiritual healing, calling on elementals and spirits, veneration of ancient deities and archetypes as well as attunement with the forces of nature. Today, both men and women are equally termed 'witches.' We hope that the reader is inspired by this incredibly short history of the folklore surrounding witchcraft, to find out more about this intriguing subject.

[90] MORE WONDERS

OF THE

INVISIBLE WORLD.

PART V.

An Impartial Account of the moſt Memorable Matters of Faſt, touching the ſuppoſed Witchcraft in New-England.

MR. *PARRIS*[1] had been ſome years a Miniſter in *Salem-Village*, when this ſad Calamity (as a deluge) overflowed them, ſpreading

[1] The following Entry is in the Hand-writing of Mr. Parris on his *Church Records:* "It is well known that when theſe Calamities firſt began, which was in my own Family, the Affliction was ſeveral Weeks before ſuch helliſh Operations as Witchcraft was ſuſpected; Nay, it never broke forth to any conſiderable Light, until diabolical Means was uſed, by the making of a Cake by my Indian Man [John], who had his Directions from this our Siſter Mary Sibly. Since which Apparitions have been plenty, and exceeding much Miſchief hath followed. But by this Means (it ſeems) the Devil hath been raiſed amongſt us, and his Rage is vehement and terrible; and when he ſhall be ſilenced, the Lord only knows."—*Hanſon's Hiſt. Danvers,* 289. As will be ſeen, Mr. Parris was made Scribe at the Examination.

itfelf far and near : He was a Gentleman of Liberal Education, and not meeting with any great Encouragement, or Advantage in Merchandizing, to which for fome time he apply'd himfelf, betook himfelf to the work of the. Miniftry; this Village being then vacant, he met with fo much Encouragement, as to fettle in that Capacity among them.

After he had been there about two years, he obtained a Grant from a part of the Town, that the Houfe and Land he Occupied, and which had been Alotted by the whole People to the Miniftry, fhould be and remain to him, &c. as his own Eftate in Fee Simple. This occafioned great *Divifions* both between the Inhabitants themfelves, and between a confiderable part of them and their faid Minifter, which Divifions were but as a beginning or *Præludium* to what immediately followed.

It was the latter end of *February* 1691,[2] when divers young Perfons belonging to Mr. *Parris's* Family, and one or more of the Neighbourhood, began to [91] Act, after a ftrange & unufual manner, *viz.* as by getting into Holes, and creeping under Chairs and Stools, and to ufe fundry odd Poftures and Antick Geftures, uttering foolifh, ridiculous Speeches, which neither they

[2] It is remarkable that this Cafe fhould not be noticed in the *Wonders of the Invifible World.* It is told in Lawon's *Narrative, Page* 3. See alfo *Records of Salem Witchcraft,* 49, where by Parris's Depofition, his Age is ftated at "Thirty and nine."

themselves nor any others could make sense of; the Physicians[3] that were called could assign no reason for this; but it seems one of them, having ·recourse· to the old shift, told them he was afraid they were Bewitched; upon such suggestions, they that were concerned, applied themselves to Fasting and Prayer, which was attended not only in their own private Families, but with calling in the help of others.

March the 11*th.* Mr. *Parris* invited several Neighbouring Ministers to join with him in keeping a Solemn day of Prayer at his own House; the time of the exercise those Persons were for the most part silent, but after any one Prayer was ended, they would Act and Speak strangely and Ridiculously, yet were such as had been well Educated and of good Behaviour, the one a Girl of 11 or 12 years old, would sometimes seem to be in a *Convulsion* Fit, her Limbs being twisted several ways, and very stiff, but presently her Fit would be over.

A few days before this Solemn day of Prayer, Mr. *Parris's Indian* Man and Woman made a Cake of Rye Meal, with the Childrens Water, and Baked it in the Ashes, and as is said, gave it to the Dog; this was done as a means to Discover Witchcraft; soon after which those ill

[3] None of the Accounts give the Names of the "Physicians." "One or two of the First that were Afflicted, Complaining of unusual Illness their Relations used Physic for their *Cure*, but it was altogether in vain."—*Lawson, Second Edition,* 97-8.

affected or afflicted Perfons named feveral that they faid they faw, when in their Fits, afflicting of them.

The firft complain'd of, was the faid *Indian* Woman, named *Tituba*,[4] fhe confeffed that the *Devil* urged her to fign a Book, which he prefented to her, and alfo to work Mifchief to the Children, &c. She was afterwards Committed to Prifon, and lay there till Sold for her Fees. The account fhe fince gives of it is, that her Mafter did beat her and otherways abufe her, to make her confefs and accufe (fuch as he call'd) her Sifter-Witches, and that whatfoever fhe faid by way of confeffing or accufing others, was the effect of fuch ufage; her Mafter refufed to pay her Fees, unlefs fhe would ftand to what fhe had faid.

The Children complained likewife of two other Women, to be the Authors of their Hurt, *Viz. Sarah Good*, who had long been counted a *Melancholy* or *Diftracted* Woman, and one *Ofburn*, an Old *Bed-rid* Women, which two were Perfons fo ill thought of, that the accufation was the more readily believed; and after Examination before two *Salem* Magiftrates were committed :[5]

[4] She is faid to have been a Slave, formerly in New Spain. When arrefted and fearched, the Marks on her Body produced by the Sting of the Spaniard's Whip, were faid to be made by the Devil.—*Hanfon, Hift. Danvers*, 273. Her firft Examination was on the 1ft of March, 1691-2. It occupies four full Pages of Foolfcap, and is in the Editor's poffeffion, and has never been publifhed. There is no copy at Salem, probably, as it does not appear in Mr. Woodward's Publication.

[5] The two Magiftrates were John Hathorne and Jonathan Corwin.

March the 19*th*, Mr. *Lawfon* (who had been formerly a Preacher at the faid Village) came thither, and hath fince fet forth in Print an account of what then paffed, about which time, as he faith, they complained of Goodwife *Cory*, and Goodwife *Nurfe*, Members of Churches at the Village, and at *Salem*, many others being by that time Accufed.

March the 21*ft*, Goodwife *Cory*[6] was examined before the Magiftrates of *Salem*, at the Meeting Houfe in the Village, a throng of Spectators being prefent to fee the Novelty. Mr. *Noyes*,[7] one of the Minifters of *Salem* began with Prayer, after which the Prifoner being call'd, in order to anfwer to what [92] fhould be Alledged againft

William Allen, John Hughes, William Good and Samuel Braybrook were Witneffes againft Sarah Good. Allen fwore, that on the 1ft of March, in the Night, he faw a ftrange and unufual Beaft lying on the Ground, which, when he came up to it, it vanifhed away; and in the Place thereof, ftarted up two or three Women, who fled, though not as other Women, and foon vanifhed out of Sight. It was about an Hour within Night, and he took the Women to be Sarah Good, Sarah Ofborn, and Tittabe. John Hughes was with him and fwore likewife. See *Records S. W.*, i, 38, where much more of the fame Tenor may be feen.

[6] Martha Cory was witneffed againft by Edward Putnam and Henry Keney, at the Commencement; and the Mittimus fets forth that fhe is the Wife of Giles Cory, of Salem Farms. At the fame Time were committed Rebecka Nurfe, Wife of Francis Nurfe, of Salem Village, Hufbandman; Dorothy Good, Daughter of William Good; Sarah Cloyce, the Wife of Peter Cloyce, of Salem Village; John Proctor, of Salem Farms, and Elizabeth his Wife. They were charged with afflicting Ann Putnam, Daughter of Thomas Putnam, Abigail Williams, Elizabeth Hubbard, and others.

[7] Nicholas Noyes was Son of Nicholas Noyes, of Newbury, a Graduate of H. C., 1667, and died in 1717. He was one of the fevereft Inftigators of the Proceedings againft the accufed Perfons. He was fettled in Salem in 1683.

her, fhe defired that fhe might go to Prayer, and was anfwered by the Magiftrates, that they did not come to hear her pray, but to examine her. The number of the Afflicted were at that time about Ten, *Viz.* Mrs. *Pope*, Mrs. *Putman*, good-wife *Bibber*,[8] and Goodwife *Goodall, Mary Wol-cott, Mercy Lewes* (at *Thomas Putmans*) and Dr. *Griggs* Maid, and three Girls, *Viz. Elizabeth Par-ris*, Daughter to the Minifter, *Abigail Williams* his Neice, and *Ann Putman*, which laft three, were not only the beginners, but were alfo the chief in thefe Accufations.[9] Thefe Ten were

[8] Indifferently written in the Records *Bibber* and *Vibber*. The true Name appears to be *Bibber*. Sarah Bibber, in her Teftimony againft Sarah Good, gives her Age as 36. She gave Evidence againft nine Perfons at different Times. Not much has been found about her beyond her own Teftimony. She appears to have had a Hufband, who had the Prefix Goodman. At one Time fhe and her Hufband lived at the Houfe of Jofeph Fowler. Fowler gave her a bad Character; as given to Tattling and Mifchief-making ; would call her Hufband bad Names, was "of a very tur-bulent, unruly Spirit." Alfo Tho-mas Jacobs and his Wife Mary, faid that " Good Bibbor did for a Time furgine [fojourn] in their Houfe;" that fhe "uery often fpcke-ing againft one and nother uery ob-fanely, and wichfhing [wifhing] uery bad wichchis, and uery often. She wichs that when hor chill [child]

fell into the Reuer that fhe had neuer pull hor child out." That fhe made ill Wifhes againft every-body and herfelf too. "The nay-borhud were fhe liueued amonkes aftor fhe bered hor fuft houfbon hes tolld us that this John Bibber Wife coud fall into fitts as fhe plefed."—*Records S. W.*, ii, 204-5.

Neither Felt nor Savage appear to have met with either the Name of *Bibber* or *Vibber*.

[9] "It was feveral Times obferved, that when they were difcourfed with about GOD or CHRIST, or the Things of *Salvation*, they were prefently afflicted at a dreadful Rate, and hence were oftentimes *Outra-gious*, if they were permitted to be in the Congregation, in the Time of the Publick Worfhip."—*Law-fon, Second Edit.*, 98.

"On Lord's Day, the 20th of *March* were fundry of the afflicted Perfons at Meeting, as Mrs. *Pope* [Wife of Mr. Jofeph P.], Good-

moſt of them preſent at the Examination, and did vehemently accuſe her of Afflicting them, by Biting, Pinching, Strangling, &c. And they ſaid, they did in their Fits ſee her likeneſs coming to them, and bringing a Book for them to Sign; Mr. *Hathorn*, a Magiſtrate of *Salem*, aſked her, why ſhe Afflicted thoſe Children? ſhe ſaid, ſhe did not Afflict them, he aſked her who did then? ſhe ſaid, I do not know, how ſhould I know? ſhe ſaid, they were Poor Diſtracted Creatures, and no heed to be given to what they ſaid; Mr. *Hathorn* and Mr. *Noyes* replied that it was the Judgment of all that were there preſent, that they were bewitched, and only ſhe (the Accuſed) ſaid they were Diſtracted: She was Accuſed by them, that the *Black Man* Whiſpered to her in her Ear now

---

wife *Bibber, Abigail Williams, Mary Walcut, Mary Lewes,* and Docter *Grigg's* Maid. There was alſo at Meeting Goodwife C. [Cory] (who was afterward Examined on Suſpicion of being a *Witch:*) They had ſeveral ſore Fits, in the Time of Publick Worſhip, which did ſomething interrupt me in my firſt Prayer; being ſo unuſual. After Pſalm was Sung *Abigail Williams* ſaid to me, *Now ſtand up,* and *Name your Text!* And after it was read, ſhe ſaid, *It is a long Text.* In the beginning of Sermon, Mrs. *Pope,* a Woman afflicted, ſaid to me, *Now there is enough of that.* And in the Afternoon, *Abigail Williams,* upon my referring to my Doctrine, ſaid to me, *I know no Doctrine you had, if you did name one, I have forgot it.* In Sermon Time when Goodwife C. was preſent *Ab. W.* called out, *Look where Goodwife C. ſits on the Beam ſuck*[l]*ing her Yellow Bird betwixt her Fingers! Anne Putman,* another Girle afflicted, *ſaid there was a Yellow Bird ſat on my Hat as it hung on the Pin in the Pulpit!* But thoſe that were by reſtrained her from ſpeaking loud about it."
—*Lawſon, Firſt Edition,* Pages 3 and 4.

This, as will have been noticed, is the Account of an Eye Witneſs.

(while fhe was upon Examination) and that fhe
had a Yellow Bird, that did ufe to Suck between
her Fingers, and that the faid Bird did Suck now
in the Affembly ; order being given to look in
that place to fee if there were any fign, the Girl
that pretended to fee it faid, that it was too late
now, for fhe had removed a Pin, and put it on
her Head, it was upon fearch found, that a Pin
was there fticking upright. When the Accufed
had any motion of their Body, Hands or Mouth,
the Accufers would cry out, as when fhe bit a
Lip, they would cry out of being bitten, if fhe
grafped one hand with the other, they would cry
out of being Pinched by her, and would produce
marks, fo of the other motions of her Body, as
complaining of being Preft, when fhe lean'd to
the feat next her, if fhe ftirred her Feet, they
would ftamp and cry out of Pain there. After
the hearing the faid *Cory* was committed to
Salem Prifon, and then their crying out of her
abated.

March the 24*th*, Goodwife *Nurfe* was brought
before Mr. *Hathorn* and Mr. *Curwin* (Magiftrates)
in the Meeting Houfe, Mr. *Hale*-Minifter of
Beverly, began with Prayer, after which fhe being
Accuf'd of much the fame Crimes made the like
anfwers, afferting her own Innocence with earneftnefs. The Accufers were moftly the fame,
Tho Putmans Wife, &c. complaining much. The
dreadful Shreiking from her and others, was very

amazing, which was heard at a great diftance; fhe was alfo Committed to Prifon.[10]

A Child of *Sarah Goods*, was likewife apprehended, being between 4 and 5 years Old, the Accufers faid this Child bit them, and would fhew fuch like marks, as thofe of a fmall Sett of Teeth upon their Arms, as many of the Afflicted

[10] The Warrant for the Apprehenfion of Rebecca Nurfe is dated 23 March, 169½. The Day following, the Marfhal, George Herrick, made his Return, that he had brought her to the houfe of *Nath. Ingerfal,* where fhe was in Cuftody. The Witneffes were Ann Puttnam, Jr., Abigail Williams, Mary Walcott, and Elizabeth Hubbard. Mary Walcott's Age was about 17; Elizabeth Hubbard's alfo about 17. Nothing could be too abominable for thefe Mifcreants to make up and fwear to. Mary Walcott faid, among other things, that befides being "moft grevioufly afflicted by" being bitten, pinched, and almoft choked by the Prifoner, becaufe fhe would not write in her Book, Goody N. faid fhe would kill her if fhe did not; and on the 3d of May, in the Evening the Apparition of the Prifoner told her "fhe had an Hand in the Deaths of Benjamin Holton, John Harrod, Rebekah Sheppard and feuerall others." Abigail Williams's Teftimony is much the fame. She heard the Accufed confefs (by her Apparition) the committing of feveral Murders, together with her Sifter Cloyfe; as upon old Good-n: Hanvood, Benj.

Porter and Rebek: Shepard...." Sarah Vibber, Mr. Sam: Parris, N. Ingerfoll and T. Putnam alfo teftified againft the poor aged Woman. Putnam's Age was about 40; Parris's, as before mentioned, about 39. John Putnam, Sen. (another Wit.) aged about 63. Edwd. Putnam, another, aged about 30. Another, Sarah Holton, relict of Benj. Holton. Another, Ann Putnam, Wife of Thomas, fwore to the choking by the Accufed, and to her declaring fhe would kill her, and faid fhe had killed Benj. Holton, John Fuller and Rebekah Shepard; alfo that fhe and her Sifter Cloyfe and Ed: Bifhop had killed young John Putnam's Child...... "Immediately there did appear to me fix Children in Winding-fheets, which called me Aunt..... Told me they were my Sifter Baker's Children of Bofton; and that Goody Nurs, and Miftris Cary of Charleftown, and an old deaf Woman at Bofton had murthered them. .... Alfo there appeared to me my own Sifter Bayley and three of her Children in Winding-fheets, and told me Goody Nurf had murthered them." This was all taken as good and fufficient Teftimony!

as the Child caſt its Eye upon, would complain they were in Torment; which Child they alſo Committed.

Concerning theſe that had been hitherto Examined and Committed, it is [93] among other things obſerved, by Mr. *Lawſon* (in Print[11]) that they were by the Accuſers charged, to belong to a Company that did muſter in Arms, and were reported by them to keep Days of Faſt, Thankſgiving and Sacraments; and that thoſe Afflicted (or Accuſers) did in the Aſſembly, Cure each other, even with a touch of their hand, when ſtrangled and otherways tortured, and would endeavour to get to the Afflicted to relieve them thereby (for hitherto they had not uſed the Experiment of bringing the Accuſed to touch the Afflicted, in order to their Cure) and could foretell one anothers Fits to be coming, and would ſay, look to ſuch a one, ſhe will have a Fit preſently and ſo it happened, and that at the ſame time when the Accuſed perſon was preſent, the Afflicted ſaid they ſaw her *Spectre* or likeneſs in other places of the Meeting Houſe Sucking [ſuckling] their Familiars.

The ſaid Mr. *Lawſon* being to Preach at the Village, after the Pſalm was Sung, *Abigail Williams* ſaid, *Now ſtand up and name your Text;* after it was read, ſhe ſaid, *It is a long Text.* Mrs. *Pope* in the beginning of Sermon ſaid to him, *Now there is*

---

[11] This Reference is to the firſt *and True Narrative, &c.* His Edition of Lawſon's Work, *A Brief* Account is given in Note 9.

enough of that. In Sermon, he referring to his Doctrine, *Abigail Williams* said to him, *I know no Doctrine you had, if you did name one I have forgot it.* *Ann Putman* an afflicted Girl, said, *There was a Yellow Bird sate on his Hat as it hung on the Pin in the Pulpit.*[12]

March 31, 1692. Was set apart as a day of Solem Humiliation at *Salem*, upon the Account of this Business, on which day *Abigail Williams* said, *That she saw a great number of Persons in the Village at the Administration of a Mock Sacrament, where they had Bread as read as raw Flesh, and red Drink.*[13]

April 1. *Mercy Lewis* affirmed, *That she saw a man in White, with whom she went into a Glorious Place,* viz. in her fits, *where was no Light of the Sun, much less of Candles, yet was full of Light and Brightness, with a great Multitude in White Glittering Robes, who Sang the Song in* Rev. v. 9. *and the* cx. *and* cxlix. Psalms; *And was given that she might tarry no longer in this place.* This White Man is said to have appeared several times to others of them, and to have given them notice how long it should be before they should have another Fit.[14]

April the 3*d.* Being Sacrament Day at the Village, *Sarah Cloys,* Sister to Goodwife *Nurse,* a

---

✦ 12 Lawson, *First Edition*, Page 4.

13 Lawson, Page 8. The Words *"at a House in the Village,"* are in the Original, which shows that the Witch-meeting was in that part of Salem since Danvers.

11 This Affair of the 1st of April, is an Abridgement of Lawson, Page 8, but nothing important to the present Purpose is omitted.

Member of one of the Churches, was (tho' it
feems with difficulty prevailed with to be) prefent; but being entred the place, and Mr. *Parris* naming his Text, *John* vi. 70. *Have not I
chofen you Twelve, and one of you is a Devil* (for
what caufe may reft as a doubt whether upon the
account of her Sifters being committed, or becaufe of the choice of that Text) fhe rofe up and
went out, the wind fhutting the Door forcibly,
gave occafion to fome to fuppofe fhe went out in
Anger, and might occafion a fufpicion of her;
However fhe was foon after complain'd of, examin'd and committed.[15]

April the 11*th.* By this time the number of
the Accufed and Accufers being much increafed,
was a Public Examination at *Salem*, Six of the
Magiftrates with feveral Minifters being prefent,
there appeared feveral who complain'd againft
others with hidious clamors and Screechings.
Goodwife *Proctor*[16] was brought thither, being

---

[15] The following is the Relation
by Lawfon, given in his own Words,
that the Reader may judge of his
accuracy: " The 3d of *April,* the
Lord's Day, being Sacrament Day,
at the Village, *Good. C.,* upon Mr.
Parris's naming his Text, *John,* 6,
70. *One of them is a Devil,* the
faid Good. *C.* went immediately
out of the Meetinghoufe, and flung
the door after her violently, to the
amazement of the Congregation:
She was afterwards feen by fome
in their Fits, who faid, *O Goodw.*

C. I did not think to fee you here!
(and being at their *red bread and
drink*) faid to her, *Is this a Time to
receive the Sacrament. You ran
away on the Lord's Day, and fcorned
to receive it in the Meetinghoufe, and
Is this a Time to receive it? I wonder at you!* This is the Summ of
what I either faw myfelf, or did receive Information from Perfons of
undoubted Reputation and Credit."
—*Page* 8.

[16] "On the 11th of April, 1692,
a Council was convened at Salem;

Accufed or cryed out againft; her Huf[94]band coming to attend and affift her, as there might be need, the Accufers cryed out of him alfo, and that with fo much earneftnefs, that he was Committed with his Wife. About this time befides the Experiment of the Afflicted falling at the fight, &c. they put the Accufed upon faying the Lord's Prayer, which one among them performed, except in that petition [*Deliver us from Evil*] fhe expreft it thus (*Deliver us from all Evil*) this was lookt upon as if fhe Prayed againft what fhe was now juftly under, and being put upon it again, and repeating thofe words [*Hallowed be thy name*] fhe expreft it [*Hollowed be thy Name*] this was counted a depraving the words, as fignifying to make void, and fo a Curfe rather than a Prayer, upon the whole it was concluded that fhe alfo could not fay it, &c. Proceeding in this work of examination and Commitment many were

---

at which there were prefent DEP. GOV. THOMAS DANFORTH, JAMES RUSSELL, JOHN HATHORNE, ISAAC ADDINGTON, MAJ. SAMUEL APPLETON, CAPT. SAMUEL SEWALL and JONATHAN CORWIN. To them Complaint was exhibited by Capt. Jonathan Wallcott and Lieut. Nathaniell Ingerfall, both of Salem Village, on the behalf of feveral Neighbors, as well as on their own; againft Sarah Cloyce, wife of Peter Cloyce of Salem Village, and Elizabeth Proctor, wife of John Proctor of Salem Farms [on the Road towards Bofton] for high fufpition of fundry Acts of Witchcraft, committed on the Bodies of Abigail Williams and John Indian, both of Mr. Samuel Parris his Famyly, Mary Walcot, Ann Putnam and Mercy Lewis, &c." When the Accufed were brought before the Council, Mr. Parris "was defired and appointed to wright ye Examination," which he accepted, and the Record is ftill extant in his Hand-writing. Accordingly Elizabeth Proctor, and her Hufband, John Proctor, and Sarah Cloyce were all committed to Prifon, "per advife of ye Councill."—*Witchcraft Records*, i. 101-2.

fent to Prifon.   As an Inftance, fee the following
Mittimus :

To their Majefties Goal-keeper in *Salem.*

YOU *are in Their Majefties Names hereby required to take into your care, and fafe cuftody,
the Bodies of* William Hobs, *and* Deborah *his
Wife,* Mary Eafty, *the Wife of* Ifaac Eafty, *and*
Sarah Wild, *the Wife of* John Wild, *all of* Topf-
field ; *and* Edward Bifhop, *of* Salem-Village ;
Hufbandman, *and* Sarah *his Wife, and* Mary Black,
a negro *of Lieutenant* Nathaniel Putmans, *of* Salem-Village ; *alfo* Mary Englifh *the Wife of* Philip
Englifh,[17] *Merchant in* Salem ; *who ftand charged
with High Sufpicion of Sundry Acts of Witchcraft,*

[17] The Teftimony and Indictment againft Philip Englifh may be
feen in the *Hift. and Antiq's Bofton,*
497, printed from the Originals in
the Author's Poffeffion. With the
fame are the two Indictments (in
the Hand-writing of Edward Rawfon), charging him with bewitching
Elizabeth Booth, of Salem, Single-
woman, and Mary Wallcott. Thefe
Indictments are both dated May
31ft, 1692. The Monfters who
carried on the Charges, were much
like a Pack of hungry Wolves.
One would fet up the Howl of
Witch, and immediately others
would follow. So in the Cafe of
Philip Englifh, a large number of
Perfons joined thofe Girls in their
" Crying out on" him. This encouraged them to keep up their De-
ceptions.   Mrs. Englifh was accufed before her Hufband.   One
Mary Warren, Servant to Mr.
Procter, outwent all others, except
perhaps Elizabeth Booth, in the
Invention of Stories. Rebutting
Teftimony was brought againft her,
but it had no Effect with the Court.
Edward Bifhop, aged 44; Sarah,
41, and Mary Eftey, 56; all faid
that they heard Mary Warren fay,
when in Jail together in Salem, that
the Magiftrates might as well examine Keyfar's Daughter that had
been diftracted many Years, and
believe what fhe faid, as well as
what any of the Afflicted faid. Mary
Englifh, aged 39, faid, being at Salem about a Month before, fhe
heard Mary Warren fpeak the fame
Words.

done or committed by them lately upon the Bodies of Ann Putman, Mary Lewis *and* Abigail Williams, *of* Salem-Village ; *whereby great Hurt and Damage hath been done to the Bodies of the said Persons, according to the complaint of* Thomas Putnam *and* John Buxton *of* Salem-Village, *Exhibited.* Salem, Apr 21, 1692, *appears, whom you are to secure in order to their further Examination. Fail not.*

John Hathorn, ⎫ *Assistants.*
Jona. Curwin, ⎬
Dated Salem, April 22, 1692.

To Marshall George Herrick *of Salem Essex.* ⎫
⎬

YOU are in their Majesties Names hereby required to convey the above-named to the Goal at Salem. *Fail not.*

John Hathorn, ⎫ *Assistants,*
Jona. Curwin, ⎬
Dated Salem, Apr 22, 1692.

The occasion of *Bishops* being cry'd out of, was he being at an Examination in *Salem*, when at the Inn an afflicted *Indian* was very unruly, whom he undertook, and so managed him, that he was very orderly, after which in riding home, in company of him and other Accusers, the *Indian* fell into a fit, and clapping hold with his Teeth on the back of the Man that rode before him, thereby held

C3

himself upon the Horfe, but faid, *Bifhop* ftriking him with his ftick, the *Indian* foon recovered, and promifed he would do fo no more; to which *Bifhop* replied, that he [95] doubted not, but he could cure them all, with more to the fame effect; immediately after he was parted from them, he was cried out of, *&c.*

May 14, 1692. Sir *William Phips* arrived with Commiffion from their Majefties to be Governor, purfuant to the New Charter; which he now brought with him; the Ancient Charter having been vacated by King *Charles,* and King James (by which they had a power not only to make their own Laws; but alfo to chufe their own Governor and Officers;) and the Countrey for fome years was put under an abfolute Commiffion-Government, till the Revolution, at which time, tho more than two thirds of the People were for reafuming their ancient Government, (to which they had encouragement by his then Royal High-nefs's Proclamation) yet fome that might have been better imployed[18] (in another Station) made

---

[18] Dr. Mather affirms that "the *Old Government* was *Reafumed,* and the *Old Charter* too was *Reafumed,* as far as it was poffible to be done; Every thing in the World was done, but only declaring that the *Judgment* paffed in the King's Court of Chancery (however it might be thought a Grievance) did the *Charter* no *Damage;* which if fome were wifer then to fay, who can help it? Well, did I oppofe this *Reafumption!* They that were acquainted with me, I am fure, did not think fo; and they that fent their *Tory Pamphlets* about the Countrey againft me, as an *Impudent Youth* [then aged 26] for my affifting the *Reafumed Government,* I am fure did not think fo. Let the things Publifhed for the fupporting of the Reafumed Government; and particularly the very firft *Paffage* in the *firft Sermon,* at the

it their bufinefs (by printing, as well as fpeaking)
to their utmoft to divert them from fuch a fettlement; and fo far prevailed, that for about feven
Weeks after the Revolution, here was not fo
much as a face of any Government; but fome
few Men upon their own Nomination would be
called a Committee of Safety; but at length the
Affembly prevailed with thofe that had been of
the Government, to promife that they would reaffume; and accordingly a Proclamation was
drawn, but before publifhing it, it was underwritten, that they would not have it underftood
that they did reaffume Charter-Government; fo
that between Government and no Government,
this Countrey remained till Sir *William* arrived:
Agents being in this time impowered in *England*,
which no doubt did not all of them act according
to the Minds or Interefts of thofe that impowered
them, which is manifeft by their not acting
jointly in what was done; fo that this place is
perhaps a fingle Inftance (even in the beft of
Reigns) of a Charter not reftored after fo happy
a Revolution.[19]

Anniverfary Election, which the Deputies of the *General-Court* called
me to *Preach* and *Print,* (which
by the way, would they have done,
if the *Young Man* had been fuch
an one as this Man would render
him?) be my Everlafting Apology;
and let *Calves* never Bleat, nor
Bulls (of *Bafhan*) Roar againft me,
on that Point any more."—*Remarks upon a Scandalous Book,* &c.,
Pages 46-7. The "Paffage" he
refers to in his Election Sermon is
too long to be extracted here.

[19] Our Author is not the only
one who thought Dr. I. Mather
had fome felfifh Ends to anfwer in
his Management of Affairs in England. See Quincy, *Hift. H. Col.,*
i, 60. But Qnincy is entirely too
one-fided, ardent and dogmatical to
be implicitly relied upon.

This fettlement by Sir *William Phips* his being come Governour put an end to all difputes of thefe things,[20] and being arrived, and having read his Commiffion, the firft thing he exerted his Power in, was faid to be his giving Orders that Irons fhould be put upon thofe in Prifon; for tho for fometime after thefe were Committed, the Accufers ceafed to cry out of them; yet now the cry againft them was renewed, which occafioned fuch Order; and tho there was partiality in the executing it (fome having taken them off almoft as foon as put on) yet the cry of thefe Accufers againft fuch ceafed after this Order.[21]

May 24. Mrs. *Cary* of *Charleftown*, was Examined and Committed. Her Hufband Mr. *Nathaniel Cary* has given account thereof, as alfo of her Efcape, to this Effect,

I having heard fome days, that my Wife was accufed of Witchcraft, being much difturbed at it, by advice, we went to Salem-Village, *to fee if the af*[96]*flicted knew her; we arrived there,* 24. *May, it happened to be a day appointed for Examination;*

---

[20] That is the Difputes refpecting the Form of Government.

[21] It appears that fome Irons had been prepared before the Arrival of Gov. Phips, though he may have ordered a further Supply, as Prifoners greatly increafed about that Time. Mr. Felt, the Annalift of Salem, furnifhed Mr. J. W. Hanfon with a Copy of an Account of the Prifon-keeper (John Arnold), of Bofton, for various Items ufed in the Prifon. Said Account begins about the 7th of March, 1691-2. On "May 9th, To Chains for Sarah Good and Sarah Ofborn, 14 *s.* May 23d, To Shackles for 10 Prifoners. May 29th, to 1 pr. Irons for Mary Cox," &c. See *Hift. Danvers*, 290. For other Items of this Sort, fee *Records of S. W.*, ii, 212, *et feq.*

accordingly foon after our arrival, Mr. Hathorn
and Mr. Curwin, &c. *went to the Meeting-houfe,
which was the place appointed for that Work, the
Minifter began with Prayer, and having taken care
to get a convenient place, I obferved, that the afflicted were two Girls of about Ten Years old, and
about two or three other, of about eighteen, one of
the girls talked moft, and could difcern more than the
reft. The Prifoners were called in one by one, and
as they came in were cried out of, &c. The Prifoner was placed about 7 or 8 foot from the Juftices,
and the Accufers between the Juftices and them;
the Prifoner was ordered to ftand right before the
Juftices, with an Officer appointed to hold each hand,
leaft they fhould therewith afflict them, and the Prifoner's Eyes muft be conftantly on the Juftices; for if
they look'd on the afflicted, they would either fall into
their Fits, or cry out of being hurt by them; after
Examination of the Prifoners, who it was afflicted
thefe Girls, &c. they were put upon faying the
Lord's Prayer, as a tryal of their guilt; after the
afflicted feem'd to be out of their Fits, they would
look fteadfaftly on fome one perfon, and frequently not
fpeak; and then the Juftices faid they were ftruck
dumb, and after a little time would fpeak again;
then the Juftices faid to the Accufers, which of you
will go and touch the Prifoner at the Bar? then
the moft courageous would adventure, but before they
had made three fteps would ordinarily fall down as
in a Fit; the Juftices ordered that they fhould be
taken up and carried to the Prifoner, that fhe might*

*touch them; and as soon as they were touched by the
accused, the Justices would say, they are well, before
I could discern any alteration; by which I observed
that the Justices understood the manner of it. Thus
far I was only as a Spectator, my Wife also was
there part of the time, but no notice taken of her by
the afflicted, except once or twice they came to her
and asked her name.*

But I having an opportunity to Discourse Mr.
Hale (*with whom I had formerly acquaintance*) *I
took his advice, what I had best to do, and desired of
him that I might have an opportunity to speak with
her that accused my Wife; which he promised
should be, I acquainting him that I reposed my trust
in him.*

*Accordingly he came to me after the Examination
was over, and told me I had now an opportunity to
speak with the said Accuser, viz.* Abigail Williams,
a Girl of 11 *or* 12 *Years old; but that we could
not be in private at Mr.* Parris's *House, as he had
promised me; we went therefore into the* Alehouse,
*where an Indian man attended us, who it seems was
one of the afflicted: to him we gave some Cyder, he
shewed several Scars, that seemed as if they had been
long there, and shewed them as done by Witchcraft,
and acquainted us that his Wife, who also was a
Slave, was imprison'd for Witchcraft.*[22]   *And now*

---

[22] This was *Tituba*, of whom
Mention has been before made.
See *Note* 4. Her first Examination
is a surprising Document, not only
for its Length, but for its Matter;
and the Editor cannot but candidly
confess that the Questions were more
ridiculous than the Answers of the
simple Indian Woman, if possible.
Her Husband was known as *John
Indian.* The original Minutes are
in the Editor's Possession.

*inſtead of one Accuſer, they all came in, who began
to tumble down like Swine, and then three Women
were called in to attend them. We in the Room
were all at a ſtand, to ſee who they would cry out
of; but in a ſhort time they cried* [97] *out,* Cary :
*and immediately after a Warrant was ſent from the
Juſtices to bring my Wife before them, who were
ſitting in a Chamber near by, waiting for this.*

*Being brought before the Juſtices, her chief ac-
cuſers were two* Girls: *my Wife declared to the
Juſtices, that ſhe never had any knowledge of them
before that day ; ſhe was forced to ſtand with her
Arms ſtretched out. I did requeſt that I might hold
one of her hands, but it was denied me ; then ſhe
deſired me to wipe the Tears from her Eyes, and the
Sweat from her Face, which I did; then ſhe deſired
ſhe might lean herſelf on me, ſaying, ſhe ſhould faint.*

Juſtice Hathorn *replied, ſhe had ſtrength enough
to torment thoſe perſons, and ſhe ſhould have ſtrength
enough to ſtand. I ſpeaking ſomething againſt their
cruel proceedings, they commanded me to be ſilent, or
elſe I ſhould be turned out of the Room. The Indian
before mentioned, was alſo brought in to be one of her
Accuſers : being come in, he now (when before the
Juſtices) fell down and tumbled about like a Hog,
but ſaid nothing. The Juſtices aſked the Girls,
who afflicted the Indian ? they anſwered ſhe (meaning my wife) and now lay upon him; the Juſtices
ordered her to touch him, in order to his cure, but
her head muſt be turned another way, leaſt inſtead of
curing, ſhe ſhould make him worſe, by her looking on*

*him, her hand being guided to take hold of his; but
the Indian took hold on her hand, and pulled her
down on the Floor, in a barbarous manner; then his
hand was taken off, and her hand put on his, and the
cure was quickly wrought.   I being extreamly troubled at their Inhumane dealings, uttered a hafty
Speech* [That God would take vengeance on them,
and defired that God would deliver us out of the
hands of unmerciful men.]   *Then her Mittimus
was writ; I did with difficulty and charge obtain
the liberty of a Room, but no beds in it; if there
had, could have taken but little reft that Night, fhe
was committed to Bofton Prifon; but I obtained a
Habeas Corpus to remove her to Cambridge Prifon,
which is in our County of Middlefex.   Having been
there one Night, next Morning the Jaylor*[23] *put
Irons on her legs (having received fuch a command)
the weight of them was about eight pounds; thefe
with her other Afflictions, foon brought her into Con-
vulfion Fits, fo that I thought fhe would have died
that Night, I fent to intreat that the Irons might be
taken off, but all intreaties were in vain, if it would
have faved her Life, fo that in this condition fhe
muft continue.   The Tryals at Salem coming on, I
went thither, to fee how things were managed; and
finding that the Spectre-Evidence was there received,
together with Idle, if not Malicious ftories, againft
Peoples Lives, I did eafily fee which way it would
go; for the fame Evidence that ferved for one, would*

---

[23] This application of Irons was
of courfe after the Arrival of the
Governor. The Name of the Jailor
has already been given.

*ferve for all the reft; I acquainted her with her
danger; and that if fhe were carried to Salem to be
tried, I feared fhe would never return. I did my
utmoft that fhe might have her Tryal in our own
County, I with feveral others Petitioning the Judge
for it, and were put in hopes of it;* [98] *but I foon
faw fo much, that I underftood thereby it was not
intended, which put me upon confulting the means of
her efcape; which thro the goodnefs of God was
effected, and fhe got to Road Ifland, but foon found
herfelf not fafe when there, by reafon of the purfuit
after her; from thence fhe went to New-York, along
with fome others that had efcaped their cruel hands;
where we found his Excellency* Benjamin Fletcher,
*Efq: Governour, who was very courteous to us. Af-
ter this fome of my Goods were feized in a Friends
hands, with whom I had left them, and myfelf imprifoned by the Sheriff, and kept in Cuftody half a
day, and then difmift; but to fpeak of their ufage of
the Prifoners, and their Inhumanity fhewn to them, at
the time of their Execution, no fober Chriftian could
bear; they had alfo tryals of cruel mockings; which
is the more, confidering what a People for Religion,
I mean the profeffion of it, we have been; thofe that
fuffered being many of them Church-Members, and
moft of them unfpotted in their Converfation, till
their Adverfary the Devil took up this Method for
accufing them.*

Per Jonathan Cary.[24]

---

[24] It would feem from the *Re-
cords,* (as publifhed by Mr. Wood-   ward) that Cary's name was *Nathaniel.* In Savage, we find that

May 31. Captain *John Aldin* was Examined at *Salem*, and Committed to *Boſton* Priſon, the Priſon-Keeper ſeeing ſuch a Man Committed, of whom he had a good eſteem, was after this the more Compaſſionate to thoſe that were in Priſon on the like account; and did refrain from ſuch hard things to the Priſoners, as before he had uſed. Mr. *Aldin* himſelf has given account of his Examination, in theſe Words.

An Account how John Aldin,[25] *Senior, was dealt with at* Salem-*Village.*

JOHN ALDIN *Senior, of Boſton, in the County of Suffolk, Marriner, on the 28th Day of May,* 1692, *was ſent for by the Magiſtrates of* Salem, *in the County of Eſſex, upon the Accuſation of a company of poor diſtraƈted, or poſſeſſed Creatures or Witches; and being ſent by Mr.* Stoughton, *arrived there the* 31ſt of May, *and appeared at* Salem-Village, *before Mr.* Gidney, *Mr.* Hathorn, *and Mr.* Curwin.

Jonathan Cary of Charleſtown had Wife Hannah Winſor; that *Nathaniel* was Brother to Jonathan, and that they were Sons to James Cary, who came to Charleſtown in or before 1639, Complaint was made againſt Mrs. Cary by Mr. Thomas Putnam and Benjamin Hatchinſon, both of.Salem Village. The Complaint was that ſhe had bewitched the miſcreant Girls before-mentioned, Mary Walcott, Abigall Willyams and Mercy Lewis. Mrs. Cary's Huſband is ſtyled "Capt. Nathaniell Cary of Charls Towne, Marener."—*Records, ii.,* 196.

[25] He was the Son of the Pilgrim John of the Mayflower. See an Account of him and his Perſecution in *Hiſt. and Antiqs. Boſton,* 499. Alſo *Records S. W.,* ii., 196. His Accuſers were the ſame Wretches—Mary Lewis, Abigail Williams, Elizabeth Booth, Mary Walcott, Elizabeth Hubbard, Ann Putnam and Mary Warren. The Warrant for his Commitment was dated May 31ſt, 1692, as will be ſeen immediately onward.

Thoſe Wenches being preſent, who plaid their jugling tricks, falling down, crying out, and ſtaring in Peoples Faces; the Magiſtrates demanded of them ſeveral times, who it was of all the People in the Room that hurt them? one of theſe *Accuſers pointed ſeveral times at one* Captain Hill,[26] *there preſent, but ſpake nothing; the ſame Accuſer, had a Man ſtanding at her back to hold her up; he ſtooped down to her Ear, then ſhe cried out,* Aldin, Aldin *afflicted her; one of the Magiſtrates aſked her if ſhe had ever ſeen* Aldin, *ſhe anſwered no, he aſked how ſhe knew it was* Aldin? *She ſaid, the Man told her ſo.*

Then all were ordered to go down into the Street, where a Ring was made; and the ſame Accuſer cried out, there ſtands Aldin, *a bold fellow with his Hat on before the Judges, he ſells Powder and Shot to the* Indians *and* French, [99] *and lies with the* Indian *Squaes, and has* Indian *Papooſes. Then was* Aldin *committed to the Marſhal's Cuſtody, and his Sword taken from him; for they ſaid he afflicted them with his Sword. After ſome hours* Aldin *was ſent for to the Meeting-houſe in the Village before the Magiſtrates; who required* Aldin *to ſtand upon a Chair, to the open view of all the People.*

The Accuſers cried out that Aldin *did pinch them, then, when he ſtood upon the Chair, in the ſight of all the People, a good way diſtant from them, one of the Magiſtrates bid the Marſhal to hold open* Aldins *hands, that he might not pinch thoſe Creatures.* Aldin *aſked them why they ſhould think, that he ſhould come*

---

[26] The ſame, probably, mentioned before. See Vol. ii, Page 75.

to that *Village* to afflict *thofe perfons that he never knew or faw before?* Mr. Gidney *bid* Aldin *confefs, and give glory to God:* Aldin *faid he hoped he fhould give glory to God, and hoped he fhould never gratifie the Devil; but appealed to all that ever knew him, if they ever fufpected him to be fuch a perfon, and challenged any one, that could bring in any thing upon their own knowledge, that might give fufpicion of his being fuch an one.* Mr. Gidney *faid he had known* Aldin *many Years, and had been at Sea with him, and always look'd upon him to be an honeft Man, but now he did fee caufe to alter his judgment:* Aldin *anfwered, he was forry for that, but he hoped God would clear up his Innocency, that he would recall that judgment again, and added that he hoped that he fhould with* Job *maintain his Integrity till he died. They bid* Aldin *look upon the Accufers, which he did, and then they fell down.* Aldin *afked Mr.* Gidney, *what reafon there could be given, why* Aldin's *looking upon him did not ftrike him down as well? but no reafon was given that I heard. But the Accufers were brought to* Aldin *to touch them, and this touch they faid made them well.* Aldin *began to fpeak of the Providence of God, in fuffering thefe Creatures to accufe Innocent perfons;* Mr. Noyes *afked* Aldin *why he would offer to fpeak of the Providence of God, God by his Providence (faid Mr.* Noyes) *governs the World, and keeps it in peace; and fo went on with Difcourfe, and ftopt* Aldin's *mouth, as to that.* Aldin *told Mr.* Gidney, *that he could affure him that there was a lying Spirit in them, for I can aſſure you that there is not a word of truth in all theſe ſay of me. But Aldin was again committed to the Marſhal, and his Mittimus written, which was as follows.*

To Mr. John Arnold, Keeper of the Priſon in Boſton, *in the County of* Suffolk.[27]

WHEREAS *Captain* John Aldin *of* Boſton, *Mariner, and* Sarah Rice, *Wife of* Nicholas Rice *of* Reding, *Huſbandman, have been this day brought before us,* John Hathorn *and* Jonathan Curwin, *Eſquires; being accuſed and ſuſpeȼted of perpetrating divers aȼts of Witchcraft, contrary to the form of the Statute, in that Caſe made and provided: Theſe are therefore* [100] *in Their Majeſties,* King William *and* Queen Marys *Names, to Will and require you, to take into your Cuſtody, the bodies of the ſaid* John Aldin, *and* Sarah Rice, *and them ſafely keep, until they ſhall thence be delivered by due courſe of Law; as you will anſwer the contrary at your peril; and this ſhall be your ſufficient Warrant. Given under our hands at* Salem-Village, *the* 31ſt *of* May, *in the Fourth Year of the Reign of our Sovereign Lord and Lady,* William *and* Mary, *now King and Queen over* England, &c, *Anno Dom.* 1692.

John Hathorn, } *Aſſiſtants.*
Jonathan Curwin, }

27 The original Mittimus does not appear among the Records preſerved at Salem. If preſerved, it has not been diſcovered.

To Bofton Aldin *was carried by a Conflable, no Bail would be taken for him; but was delivered to the Prifon-keeper, where he remained Fifteen Weeks; and then obferving the manner of Tryals, and Evidence then taken, was at length prevailed with to make his Efcape, and being returned, was bound over to Anfwer at the Superior Court at* Bofton, *the laft* Tuefday *in* April, Anno, 1693. *And was there cleared by Proclamation, none appearing againft him.*

Per. John Aldin.

At Examination, and at other times, 'twas ufual for the Accufers to tell of the black Man, or of a Spectre, as being then on the Table, &c. The People about would ftrike with Swords, or fticks at thofe places. One Juftice broke his cane at this Exercife, and fometimes the Accufers would fay, they ftruck the Spectre, and it is reported feveral of the accufed were hurt and wounded thereby, though at home at the fame time.

The Juftices proceeding in thefe works of Examination, and Commitment, to the end of *May*, there was by that time about a Hundred perfons Imprifoned upon that Account.[28]

June 2. A fpecial Commiffion of *Oyer* and *Terminer*, having been Iffued out, to Mr. *Stoughton*, the New Lieutenant Governour, Major *Saltonftall*, Major *Richards*, Major *Gidny*, Mr. *Wait Winthrop*,

---

[28] Their Names may, probably, nearly all be collected from the Records. Intereft fhould prompt fome one to make the Attempt.

Captain *Sewall,* and Mr. *Sergeant ;*[29] Thefe (a
Quorum of them) fat at *Salem* this day ; where the
moft that was done this Week, was the Tryal of
one *Bifhop* alias *Oliver,* of *Salem;* who having long
undergone the repute of a Witch, occafioned by
the Accufations of one *Samuel Gray:* he about
20 Years fince, having charged her with fuch
Crimes, and though upon his Death-bed, he teftified his forrow and repentance for fuch Accufations, as being wholly groundlefs ; yet the report
taken up by his means continued, and fhe being
accufed by thofe afflicted, and upon fearch a Tet,
as they call it, being found, fhe was brought in
guilty by the Jury ; fhe [101] received her Sentence of Death, and was Executed, *June* 10. but
made not the leaft Confeffion of any thing relating
to Witchcraft.[30]

June 15. Several Minifters in and near *Bofton,*
having been to that end confulted by his Excellency, expreft their minds to this effect, *viz.*

That they were affected with the deplorable
ftate of the afflicted; That they were thankful
for the diligent care of the Rulers, to detect the
abominable Witchcrafts, which have been committed in the Country, praying for a perfect difcovery thereof. But advifed to a cautious proceeding, leaft many Evils enfue, *&c.* And that

---

[29] Their Names have already
appeared. Capt. Sewall was the
well known Judge Sewall.

[30] See the long and tedious Teftimonies againft her in Vol. I, Pages
163-174, and of the fame ridiculous
Character as others ; yet not fo ridiculous there as in the original
Records, which fee. Ezekiel Chee-
ver took down the Examination.

tendernefs be ufed towards thofe accufed, relating to matters prefumptive and convictive, and alfo to privacy in Examinations, and to confult Mr. *Perkins* and Mr. *Bernard*, what tefts to make ufe of in the Scrutiny : That Prefumptions and Convictions ought to have better grounds, than the Accufers affirming that they fee fuch perfons Spectres afflicting them ; and that the Devil may afflict in the fhape of good Men ; and that falling at the fight, and rifing at the touch of the Accufed, is no infallible proof of guilt ; That feeing the Devils ftrength confifts in fuch Accufations, our difbelieving them may be a means to put a . period to the dreadful Calamities ; Neverthelefs they humbly recommend to the Government, the fpeedy and vigorous profecution of fuch as have rendered themfelves obnoxious, according to the direction given in the Laws of God, and the wholefome Statutes of the *Englifh* Nation, for the Detection of Witchcraft.[31]

[31] Of this Abftract Dr. Mather fays : " His firft and main Defign is to render me odious unto the Countrey, as being one chief *Abettor* of that Opinion, That the Devils cannot afflict in the Shape of an Innocent Perfon ; and as being an *Inciter* of the Judges, to the Conviction of *Witchcrafts* upon that Opinion. It is very certain that his Confcience muft needs tell him, this is a moft *Lying Accufation*. For in my Book of *Memorable Providences*, which I writ before the Troubles at *Salem*, and even *before I was fo fully acquainted with the Wiles of Satan*, (for my faying of which, on a certain Occafion, he flouts at me) I have a whole Paragraph to caution againft *accounting a bewitched Perfons pretending to fee an Apparition of fuch or fuch an one, an Argument of their being Naughty People*. And fome of the Chief Minifters in this Land favoured that Book with their Atteftation, however my Friend Calef now Derides it." This was the Work recommended by Mr. Baxter.

This is briefly the fubftance of what may be feen more at large in *Cafes of Confcience*, (*ult.*) And one of them fince taking occafion to repeat fome part of this advice, *Wonders of the Invifible World*, p. 83. declares, (notwithftanding the Diffatisfaction of others) that if his faid Book may conduce to promote thankfulnefs to God for fuch Executions, he fhall rejoice, *&c.*

The 30th of *June*, the Court according to Adjournment again fat; five more were tried, *viz. Sarah Good* and *Rebecca Nurfe*, of *Salem-Village*; *Sufanna Martin* of *Amfbury*; *Elizabeth How* of *Ipfwich*; and *Sarah Wildes* of *Topsfield*: thefe were all condemned that Seffions, and were all Executed on the 19th of *July*.[32]

At the Tryal of *Sarah Good*, one of the afflicted fell in a Fit, and after coming out of it, fhe cried out of the Prifoner, for ftabbing her in the breaft with a Knife, and that fhe had broken the Knife in ftabbing· of her, accordingly a piece of the blade of a Knife was found about her. Immediately information being given to the Court, a young Man was called, who produced a Haft and part of the Blade, which the Court having viewed and compared, faw it to be the fame. And upon inquiry the young Man affirmed, that

[32] The Trial of Sufanna Martin is given in the *Wonders* (Vol. i.) Pages 175-187; that of Elizabeth How, Pages 188-194; that of Rebecca Nurfe in *Records of S. W.* i. 76-99; Vol. ii. 215; of Sarah Wilds of Topsfield, *Ibid*, ii, 180-182, 215; Sarah Good; *Ibid*, 11-24; ii, 214-15. The Partiality in the Wonders is elfewhere noticed.

yefterday he happened to brake that Knife, and that he caft away the upper part, this afflicted perfon being then [102] prefent, the young Man was difmift, and fhe was bidden by the Court not to tell lyes ;[33] and was improved (after as fhe had been before) to give Evidence againft the Prifoners.

At Execution, Mr. *Noyes* urged *Sarah Good* to Confefs, and told her fhe was a Witch, and fhe knew fhe was a Witch, to which fhe replied, you are a lyer ; I am no ,more a Witch than you are a Wizard, and if you take away my Life, God will give you Blood to drink.

At the Tryal of *Rebecca Nurfe*, this was remarkable that the Jury brought in their Verdict not Guilty, immediately all the accufers in the Court, and, fuddenly after all the afflicted out of Court, made an hideous out-cry, to the amazement, not only of the Spectators, but the Court alfo feemed ftrangely furprized : one of the Judges

---

[33] The Trial of Sarah Good was one of a fingularly revolting Character. Her own Daughter, named Dorothy, was one of the Witneffes againft her. Said her Mother "had three Birds, one black, one yellow, and that thefe Birds hurt the Children and afflicted Perfons."—*Records S. W.* i, 23. Her own Hufband gave her a very bad Character, but faid he knew nothing of her being a Witch. The Story of the broken Knife, I do not remember feeing in the *Records.* It was probably fuppreffed. Samuel Abbey and Mary his Wife, aged about 45 and 38, refpectively, teftified that William Good and his Wife Sarah, being deftitute of a Houfe to dwell in, they took them in out of Charity ; but about two years and a half before, were obliged to turn them out "for quietnefs fake, the faid Sarah was of fo turbulant a Sperritt, fpitefull and mallitioufly bent." Whereupon the faid Abbey in about two years loft 17 head of Cattle, befides Sheep and "Hoggs."—*Records, ib.* 24-5. See alfo Mr. Upham's *Lectures on Witchcraft.*

expreft himfelf not fatisfied, another of them as he was going off the Bench, faid they would have her Indicted anew. . The chief Judge faid he would not Impofe upon the Jury ; but intimated, as if they had not well confidered one Expreffion of the Prifoners when fhe was upon Tryal, *viz.* That when one *Hobbs*, who had confeffed her-felf to be a Witch, was brought into the Court to witnefs againft her, the Prifoner turning her head to her, faid, [*What, do you bring her? fhe is one of us*] or to that effect, this together with the Cla-mours of the Accufers, induced the Jury to go out again, after their Verdict, not Guilty. But not agreeing, they came into the Court, and fhe being then at the Bar, her words were repeated to her, in order to have had her explanation of them, and fhe making no Reply to them, they found the Bill, and brought her in Guilty ; thefe words being the Inducement to it, as the Foreman has fignified in writing, as follows.

July 4, 1692. I Thomas Fifk,[34] *the Subfcriber hereof, being one of them that were of the Jury laft week at* Salem-court, *upon the Tryal of* Rebecca Nurfe, *&c. being defired by fome of the Relations to give a Reafon why the Jury brought her in Guilty, after her Verdict not Guilty ; I do hereby give my Reafons to be as follows,* viz.

When the Verdict not Guilty was, the honored Court was pleafed to object againft it, faying to them, that

---

34 The Names of the Jurors are Foreman, Brother-in-law, I fuppofe
not recorded. John Ruck was the of Mr. Burroughs.

*they think they let flip the words, which the Prifoner
at the Bar fpake againft herfelf, which were fpoken
in reply to Goodwife* Hobbs *and her Daughter, who
had been faulty in fetting their hands to the Devils
Book, as they have confeffed formerly ; the words were*
[What do thefe perfons give in Evidence againft
me now, they ufed to come among us.] *After
the honored Court had manifefted their diffatisfaction of
the Verdict, feveral of the Jury declared themfelves
defirous to go out again, and thereupon the Honoured
Court gave leave ; but when we came to confider of
the Cafe, I could not tell how to take her words, as
an Evidence againft her, till fhe had a further opportunity to put her Senfe upon them, if fhe would
take it ; and then going into Court, I mentioned the
words aforefaid, which by one of the* [103] *Court
were affirmed to have been fpoken by her, fhe being
then at the Bar, but made no reply, nor interpretation
of them ; whereupon thefe words were to me a principal Evidence againft her.*

Thomas Fifk.

When goodwife *Nurfe* was informed what ufe was
made of thefe words, fhe put in this following
Declaration into the Court.

THESE *prefents do humbly fhew to the honoured
Court and Jury, that I being informed, that
the Jury brought me in Guilty, upon my faying that
Goodwife* Hobbs *and her Daughter were of our Company ; but I intended no otherways, than as they were*

Prifoners with us, and therefore did then, and yet do judge them not legal Evidence againft their fellow Prifoners. And I being fomething hard of hearing, and full of grief, none informing me how the Court took up my words, and therefore had no opportunity to declare what I intended, when I faid they were of our Company.

Rebecka Nurfe.

After her Condemnation fhe was by one of the Minifters of *Salem* excommunicated; yet the Governour faw caufe to grant a Reprieve, which when known (and fome fay immediately upon granting) the Accufers renewed their difmal outcries againft her, infomuch that the Governour was by fome *Salem* Gentleman prevailed with to recall the Reprieve, and fhe was Executed with the reft.

The Teftimonials of her Chriftian behaviour, both in the courfe of her Life, and at her Death, and her extraordinary care in educating her Children, and fetting them good Examples, &c. under the hands of fo many, are fo numerous, that for brevity they are here omitted.[35]

It was at the Tryal of thefe that one of the Accufers cried out publickly of Mr. *Willard* Minifter in *Bofton*, as afflicting of her, fhe was fent out of the Court, and it was told about fhe was miftaken in the perfon.

---

[35] It is much to be regretted that the Author found it neceffary to exclude fuch Documents. The Paper referred is of fpecial regret.

August 5. The Court again fitting, fix more were tried on the fame Account, viz. Mr. *George Burroughs*, fometime minifter of *Wells*, *John Procter*, and *Elizabeth Procter* his Wife, with *John Willard* of *Salem*-Village, *George Jacobs* Senior, of *Salem*, and *Martha Carryer* of *Andover;* thefe were all brought in Guilty and Condemned ; and were all Executed *Auguſt* 19, except *Procter's* Wife, who pleaded Pregnancy.[36]

Mr. *Burroughs* was carried in a Cart with the others, through the ftreets of *Salem* to Execution ; when he was upon the Ladder, he made a Speech for the clearing of his Innocency, with fuch Solemn and Serious Expreffions, as were to the Admiration of all prefent; his Prayer (which he concluded by repeating the Lord's Prayer,) was fo well worded, and uttered with fuch compofednefs, and fuch (at leaft feeming) fervency of [104] Spirit, as was very affecting, and drew Tears from many (fo that it feemed to fome, that the Spectators would hinder the Execution) the accufers faid the black Man ftood and dictated to him ; as foon as he was turned off, Mr. *Cotton Mather*, being mounted upon a Horfe, addreffed himfelf to the People, partly to declare, that he was no ordained Minifter, and partly to poffefs the People of his guilt ; faying That the Devil has often been transformed into an Angel of

---

[36] What has been preferved of the Trials of thefe Perfons, will be found in Vol. i, and in the *Records* before cited.

Light;[37] and this did fomewhat appeafe the People, and the Executions went on; when he was cut down, he was dragged by the Halter to a Hole, or Grave, between the Rocks, about two foot deep, his Shirt and Breeches being pulled off, and an old pair of Troufers of one Executed, put on his lower parts, he was fo put in, together with *Willard* and *Carryer*, one of his Hands and his Chin, and a Foot of one of them being left uncovered.

John Willard, had been imployed to fetch in feveral that were accufed; but taking diffatisfaction from his being fent, to fetch up fome that he had better thoughts of, he declined the Service, and prefently after he himfelf was accufed of the fame Crime, and that with fuch vehemency, that they fent after him to apprehend him; he had

---

[37] "I was prefent when thefe things were teftified againft him, and obferved that he could not make any Plea for himfelf (*in thefe Things*) that had any Weight: He had the Liberty of Challenging his *Jurors*, before empannelling, according to the *Statute* in that Cafe, and ufed his Liberty in Challenging many; yet the Jury that were *Sworn* brought him in Guilty."—Lawfon, *Second Edition*, 115.

Mr. Burroughs' Trial is fully given in Vo.l i, 152-63, It is not among the Records, for the Reafon, probably, that it had been given to Mr. Mather to ufe, and was never returned. His Examination was before Stoughton, Hathorne, Sewall and Corwin. The following are the Names of the Men appointed to fearch him for Teats: Edward Welch, William Gill, Zeb. Hill, Thomas Flint, Thomas Weft, Samuel Morgan and John Bare, as Printed in the *Records*, ii, 112. They reported no "Tetts" upon Mr. Burroughs.

Ann Putnam's Teftimony was ingenious, and as damning as any *Infernal Spirit* could have defired. See *Records, ib.* 113-116. Mather does not give it, but fays fuch things were evidenced; as that he had murdered fundry People. See Remarks of Mr. Upham, *Lectures*, 55.

made his Efcape as far as Nafhawag,[38] about 40 Miles from *Salem ;* yet 'tis faid thofe Accufers did then prefently tell the exact time, faying, now *Willard* is taken.

John Procter and his Wife being in Prifon, the Sheriff came to his Houfe and feized all the Goods, Provifions, and Cattle that he could come at, and fold fome of the Cattle at half price, and killed others, and put them up for the *West-Indies ;* threw out the Beer out of a Barrel, and carried away the Barrel ; emptied a Pot of Broath, and took away the Pot, and left nothing in the Houfe for the fupport of the Children : No part of the faid Goods are known to be returned. *Procter* earneftly requefted Mr. *Noyes* to pray with and for him, but it was wholly denied, becaufe he would not own himfelf to be a Witch.

During his Imprifonment he fent the following Letter, in behalf of himfelf and others.

Salem-*Prifon*, July 23, 1692.

Mr. Mather, Mr. Allen,
Mr. Moody, Mr. Willard, and
Mr. Bailey.[39]

Reverend Gentlemen.

THE *innocency of our Cafe with the Enmity of our Accufers and our Judges, and Jury, whom nothing but our Innocent Blood will ferve their*

---

[38] A mifprint, probably, for *Nafhaway.*

[39] Dr. Increafe Mather, Mr. James Allen of the Old South, Mr.

turns, having Condemned us already before our Try-
als, being ſo much incenſed and engaged againſt us
by the Devil, makes us bold to Beg and Implore your
[105] *Favourable Aſſiſtance of this our Humble*
Petition to his Excellency, that if it be poſſible our
Innocent Blood may be ſpared, which undoubtedly
otherwiſe will be ſhed, if the Lord doth not merci-
fully ſtep in. The Magiſtrates, Miniſters, Jewries,
and all the People in general, being ſo much inraged
and incenſed againſt us by the Deluſion of the Devil,
which we can term no other, by reaſon we know in
our own Conſciences, we are all Innocent Perſons.
Here are five Perſons who have lately confeſſed
themſelves to be Witches, and do accuſe ſome of us, of
being along with them at a Sacrament, ſince we were
committed into cloſe Priſon, which we know to be
Lies. Two of the 5 are (Carrier's Sons) *Young*
men, who would not confeſs any thing till they tyed
them Neck and Heels, till the Blood was ready to
come out of their Noſes, and 'tis credibly believed
and reported this was the occaſion of making them
confeſs that they never did, by reaſon they ſaid one
had been a Witch a Month, and another five Weeks,
and that their Mother had made them ſo, who has
been confined here this nine Weeks. My ſon William
Proct́er, *when he was examin'd, becauſe he would*
not confeſs that he was Guilty, when he was Inno-
cent, they tyed him Neck and Heels till the Blood

Joſhua Moody, Mr. Samuel Wil- John Bailey of the Firſt Church,
lard of the Old South, and Mr. Boſton.

*gufhed out at his Nofe, and would have kept him fo
24 Hours, if one more Merciful than the reft, had
not taken pity on him, and caufed him to be unbound.
Thefe actions are very like the Popifh Cruelties.*[40]
*They have already undone us in our Eftates, and that
will not ferve their turns, without our Innocent
Bloods. If it cannot be granted that we can have
our Trials at* Bofton, *we humbly beg that you would
evdeavour to have thefe Magiftrates changed, and
others in their rooms, begging alfo and befeeching
you would be pleafed to be here, if not all, fome of
you at our Trials, hoping thereby you may be the
means of faving the fhedding our Innocent Bloods,
defiring your Prayers to the Lord in our behalf, we
reft your Poor Afflicted Servants,*

John Procter, &c.

He pleaded very hard at Execution, for a little
refpite of time, faying that he was not fit to die;
but it was not granted.

Old *Jacobs* being Condemned, the Sheriff and
Officers came and feized all he had, his Wife had
her Wedding Ring taken from her, but with
great difficulty obtained it again. She was forced
to buy Provifions of the Sheriff, fuch as he had
taken, towards her own fupport, which not being fufficient, the Neighbours of Charity relieved
her.

---

[40] My friend Savage calls this an
"Infernal Bufinefs." I hope he will
never get further out of the Way.
It would feem that the Officials of
that Day muft have taken leffons of
Roman Inquifitors.

Margaret Jacobs being one that had confeſſed her own Guilt, and teſtified againſt her Grand-Father *Jacobs*, Mr. *Burroughs*, and *John Willard*. She the day before Executions, came to Mr. *Burroughs*, acknowledging that ſhe had belyed them, and begged Mr. *Burroughs* Forgiveneſs, who not only forgave her, but alſo Prayed with and for her. She wrote the following Letter to her Father.

From the Dungeon in *Salem* Priſon,
Auguſt 20, 1692.

Honoured Father,

AFTER *my Humble Duty Remembered to you, hoping in the Lord of your good Health, as Bleſſed be God I enjoy, tho in abundance of Affliction, being cloſe confined here in a loathſome Dungeon, the Lord look down in mercy upon me, not knowing how ſoon I ſhall be put to Death, by means of the Afflicted Perſons ; my Grand-Father having Suffered already, and all his Eſtate Seized for the King. The reaſon of my Confinement is this, I having, through the Magiſtrates Threatnings, and my own Vile and Wretched* [106] *heart, confeſſed ſeveral things contrary to my Conſcience and Knowledge, tho to the Wounding of my own Soul, the Lord pardon me for it ; but Oh! the terrors of a wounded Conſcience who can bear. But bleſſed be the Lord, he would not let me go on in my Sins, but in mercy I hope ſo my Soul would not ſuffer me to keep it in any longer, but I was forced to confeſs the truth of all before the*

*Magiſtrates, who would not believe me, but 'tis their
pleaſure to put me in here, and God knows how ſoon
I ſhall be put to death. Dear Fathers, let me beg
your Prayers to the Lord on my behalf, and ſend us
a Joyful and Happy Meeting in Heaven. My Mother poor Woman is very Crazy, and remembers her
kind Love to you, and to Uncle, viz. D. A.*[41] *So
leaving you to the protection of the Lord, I reſt
your Dutiful Daughter,*

Margaret Jacobs.

At the time appointed for her Tryal, ſhe had an
Impoſthume in her head, which was her Eſcape.
September 9. Six more were tried, and received
Sentance of Death, viz. *Martha Cory* of *Salem-
Village, Mary Eaſty* of Topsfield, *Alice Parker* and
Ann Pudeater of *Salem, Dorcas Hoar* of *Beverly,*
and *Mary Bradberry* of *Saliſbury.* September 16,
Giles Cory was preſt to Death.[42]

September 17. Nine more received Sentance of
Death, viz. *Margaret Scot* of *Rowley,* Goodwife

41 Daniel Andrew of Salem, as
I conjecture.

42 Nineteen Years after theſe Executions, the General Court of the
Province paſſed an Act declaring
null and void all the Attainders and
Judgments againſt thoſe who had
ſuffered for Witchcraft. This Act
was paſſed "upon the Humble Petition of the ſaid Perſons and of the
Children of others of them whoſe
Parents were Executed." The General Aſſembly alſo appointed a Committee " to conſider of yᵉ Damages
ſuſtained by ſundry Perſons proſecuted for Witchcraft in yᵉ Year
1692." The Committee computed
the Damage to thoſe above named
as follows : Mr. and Mrs. Cory
£21 ; Mary Eaſty £20 ; Alice Parker got nothing, but. Mary Parker
got £8 ; Nothing appears for Ann
Pudeater ; Dorcas Hoar £21 ; Mary Bradberry £20 ; ſome that ſuffered had no Repreſentative to receive the Award.

Redd of *Marblehead, Samuel Wardwell,* and *Mary Parker* of *Andover,* alfo *Abigail Falkner* of *Andover,* who pleaded Pregnancy, *Rebecca Eames* of *Boxford, Mary Lacy,* and *Ann Fofter* of *Andover,* and *Abigail Hobbs* of *Topsfield.* Of thefe Eight were Executed, *September* 22, viz. *Martha Cory, Mary Eafty, Alice Parker, Ann Pudeater, Margaret Scot, Willmet Redd, Samuel Wardwell,* and *Mary Parker.*[43]

Giles Cory pleaded not Guilty to his Indictment, but would not put himfelf upon Tryal by the Jury (they having cleared none upon Tryal) and knowing there would be the fame Witneffes againft him, rather chofe to undergo what Death they would put him to. In preffing his Tongue being preft out of his Mouth, the Sheriff with his Cane forced it in again, when he was dying. He was the firft in *New-England* that was ever preft to Death.

The Cart going to the Hill with thefe Eight to Execution, was for fome time at a fett; the afflicted and others faid, that the Devil hindered it,[44] *&c.*

Martha Cory, Wife to *Giles Cory,* protefting her Innocency, concluded her Life with an Eminent Prayer upon the Ladder.

[43] Allowances were made to the moft of thofe or their Children, as may be feen in the Records before cited.

[44] "The Hill" has ever fince been pointed out as *Witch Hill,* or more generally *Gallows Hill;* whence is had a fine view of the City of Salem. Some Account of this noted Hill might reafonably be expected in a Hiftory of Salem. The *Inftitute* fhould look to the Matter.

Wardwell having formerly confeffed himfelf Guilty, and after denied it, was foon brought upon his Tryal; his former Confeffion and Spectre Teftimony was all that appeared againft him. At Execution while he was fpeaking to the People, protefting his Innocency, the Executioner being at the fame time fmoaking Tobacco, the fmoak coming in his Face, interrupted his Difcourfe, thofe Accufers faid, the Devil hindered him with fmoak.

[107] *Mary Eafty*, Sifter alfo to *Rebecca Nurfe*, when fhe took her laft farewell of her Hufband, Children and Friends, was, as is reported by them prefent, as Serious, Religious, Diftinct, and Affectionate as could well be expreft, drawing Tears from the Eyes of almoft all prefent. It feems befides the Teftimony of the Accufers and Confeffors, another proof, as it was counted, appeared againft her, it having been ufual to fearch the Accufed for Tets; upon fome parts of her Body, not here to be named, was found an Excrefcence, which they called a Tet. Before her Death fhe put up the following Petition:

To the Honorable Judge and Bench now fitting in Judicature in Salem *and the Reverend Minifters, humbly fheweth, That whereas your humble poor Petitioner being Condemned to die, doth humbly beg of you, to take it into your Judicious and Pious Confideration, that your poor and humble Petitioner knowing my own Innocency (bleffed be the Lord for it) and feeing plainly the Wiles and Subtilty of my*

Accusers, by myself, cannot but judge charitably of others, that are going the same way with myself, if the Lord step not mightily in. I was confined a whole Month on the same account that I am now condemned for, an then cleared by the Afflicted persons, as some of your Honour know, and in two days time I was cried out upon by them, and have been confined and now am condemned to die. The Lord above knows my Innocency then, and likewise doth now, as at the great day will be known to Men and Angels. I Petition to your Honours not for my own Life, for I know I must die, and my appointed time is set; but the Lord he knows it is, if it be possible, that no more Innocent Blood be shed, which undoubtedly cannot be avoided in the way and course you go in. I question not, but your Honours do the utmost of your powers, in the discovery and detection of Witchcraft and Witches, and would not be guilty of Innocent Blood for the World; but by my own Innocency I know you are in the wrong way, the Lord in his infinite Mercy direct you in this great work, if it be his blessed will, that Innocent Blood be not shed; I would humbly beg of you, that your Honours would be pleased to Examine some of those confessing Witches, I being confident there are several of them have belyed themselves and others, as will appear, if not in this World, I am sure in the World to come, whither I am going; and I question not, but yourselves will see an alteration in these things: They say, myself and others have made a league with the Devil, we cannot con-

fefs, I know and the Lord he knows (as will *fhortly*
appear) they belye me, and *fo* I *queftion* not but they
do others; the Lord alone, who is the *fearcher* of all
hearts, knows that as I *fhall* anfwer it at the *Tri-
bunal Seat, that I know not the leaft thing of Witchcraft, therefore I cannot, I durft not belye my own
Soul.* I beg your Honours not to deny this my humble Petition, from a poor dying Innocent perfon, and
I queftion not but the Lord will give a bleffing to
your Endeavours.   Mary Efty.

[108] After Execution Mr. *Noyes* turning him
to the Bodies, faid, what a fad thing it is to fee
Eight Firebrands of Hell hanging there.[45]

In *October* 1692, One of *Wenham* complained
of Mrs. *Hale*, whofe Hufband, the Minifter of
Beverly, had been very forward in thefe Profecutions, but being fully fatisfied of his Wifes fincere
Chriftianity, caufed him to alter his Judgment;
for it was come to a ftated Controverfie, among
the *New-England* Divines, whether the Devil
could Afflict in a good Mans fhape; it feems
nothing elfe could convince him: yet when it
came fo near to himfelf, he was foon convinc'd
that the Devil might fo Afflict. Which fame
reafon did afterwards prevail with many others;
and much influenced to the fucceeding change at
Tryals.[46]

---

[45] Surely Cotton Mather never
uttered anything more inhuman.
Mr. Noyes has already been noticed.
[46] Mr. John Hale had teftified
againft fome of the Accufed; but I
do not find that when his own
Wife was accufed any Record was
made of it.

October 7. *(Edward Biſhop* and his Wife having made their Eſcape out of Priſon) this day Mr. *Corwin* the Sheriff, came and Seiz'd his Goods, and Cattle, and had it not been for his ſecond Son (who borrowed Ten Pound and gave it him) they had been wholly loſt, the Receipt follows; but it ſeems they muſt be content with ſuch a Receipt as he would give them.

Received this 7th *day of* October 1692, *of* Samuel Biſhop *of the Town of* Salem, *of the County of* Eſſex, *in* New-England, *Cordwainer, in full ſatisfaction, a valuable Sum of Money, for the Goods and Chattels of* Edward Biſhop, *Senior, of the Town and County aforeſaid, Huſbandman; which Goods and Chattels being ſeized, for that the ſaid* Edward Biſhop, *and* Sarah *his Wife, having been committed for* Witchcraft *and Felony, have made their Eſcape; and their Goods and Chattels were forfeited unto their Mageſties, and now being in Poſſeſſion of the ſaid* Samuel Biſhop; *and in behalf of their Majeſties, I do hereby diſcharge the ſaid Goods and Chattles the day and year above written, as witneſs my hand,*

George Corwin, *Sheriff.*

But before this the ſaid *Biſhops* Eldeſt Son, having Married into that Family of the *Putmans,* who were chief Proſecutors in this buſineſs; he holding a Cow to be branded left it ſhould be ſeiz'd, and having a Puſh or Boyl upon his Thigh, with his ſtraining it broke; this is that that was pretended to be burnt with the said Brand; and is one of the bones thrown to the Dogmatical to pick, in *Wonders of the Invisible World*, P. 143. the other, of a Corner of a Sheet, pretended to be taken from a Spectre, it is known that it was provided the day before, by that Afflicted person, and the third bone of a Spindle is almost as easily provided, as the piece of the Knife; so that *Apollo* needs not herein be consulted, &c.

Mr. *Philip English*,[47] and his Wife having made their Escape out of Prison, Mr. *Corwin* the Sheriff seiz'd his Estate, to the value of about Fifteen Hundred Pound, which was wholly lost to him, except about Three Hundred Pound value, (which was afterward restored.)

[109] After Goodwife *Hoar* was Condemned, her Estate was seiz'd, and was also bought again for Eight Pound.

George Jacobs, Son to old *Jacobs* being accused, he fled, then the Officers came to his House, his Wife was a Woman Crazy in her Senses and had been so several Years. She it seems had been also accused, there were in the House with her only four small Children, and one of them suck'd her Eldest Daughter, being in Prison; the Officer perswaded her out of the House, to go along with him, telling her she should speedily return, the Children ran a great way after her crying.

When she came where the Afflicted were, being

---

[47] The Case of Mr. English has been before referred to. See Note 17.

afked, they faid they did not know her, at length one faid, don't you know *Jacobs* the old Witch, and then they cry'd out of her, and fell down in their Fits; fhe was fent to Prifon, and lay there Ten Months, the Neighbours of pity took care of the Children to preferve them from perifhing.

About this time a New Scene was begun, one *Jofeph Ballard*[48] of *Andover*, whofe Wife was ill (and after died of a Fever) fent to *Salem* for fome of thofe Accufers, to tell him who afflicted his Wife; others did the like: Horfe and Man were fent from feveral places to fetch thofe Accufers who had the Spectral fight, that they might thereby tell who afflicted thofe that were any ways ill.

When thefe came into any place where fuch were, ufually they fell into a Fit; after which being afked who it was that afflicted the perfon, they would, for the moft part, name one whom they faid fat on the head, and another that fat on the lower parts of the afflicted. Soon after *Ballard*'s fending (as above) more than Fifty of the People of *Andover* were complained of, for afflicting their Neighbours. Here it was that many accufed themfelves, of Riding upon Poles through the Air; many Parents believing their Children to be Witches, and many Hufbands their Wives, *&c.* When thefe Accufers came to the Houfe of

---

[48] Ballard's Teftimony againft Samuel Wardwell may be feen in the *Records of S. W.*, ii, 152. Ballard gave his Age as about 41 Years, and mentions his Brother John. See onward.

any upon fuch account, it was ordinary for other young People to be taken in Fits, and to have the fame Spectral fight.[49]

Mr. *Dudley Bradftreet*,[50] a Juftice of Peace in *Andover*, having granted out Warrants againft, and Committed Thirty or Forty to Prifons, for the fuppofed Witchcrafts, at length faw caufe to forbear granting out any more Warrants. Soon after which he and his Wife were cried out of, himfelf was (by them) faid to have killed Nine perfons by Witchcraft, and found it his fafeft courfe to make his Efcape.

A Dog being afflicted at *Salem*-Village, thofe that had the Spectral fight being fent for, they accufed Mr. *John Bradftreet* (Brother to the Juf-

---

[49] This was not the Firft of the Troubles by fuppofed Witchcraft at Andover, as appears by the following Record, the Original of which is in the Editor's Collection: "The Depofition of Job Tylar, aged about 40 Yeares, Mary his Wife and Mofes Tyl^r his Son aged betwixt 17 and 18 Years, and Mary Tyler aboue 15 Yeares olde.—Thefe Deponents witneffe that they faw a thing like a Bird to come in at the Dore of there Houfe with John Godfery in the Night about the bignes of a Black Bird or rather bigger, to wit, as big as a Pigion, and did fly about; John Godfery labouring to catch it, and the Bird vanifhed, as they conceived, through the Chinck of a joynted Bord; and being afked by the Man of the Houfe where-

fore it came, he anfwered, It came to fuck your Wife. This was (as they remember) about 5 or 6 Yeares fince.—Taken vpon Oath of the 4 aboue menconed P ties, this 27. 4. 59. Before mee

"SIMON BRADSTREETE.
"Ouned in Court M^th, 65, by Job Tylar and Mofes Tylar.
"E. R. Sec
"Owned in Court 13 March, 65, by Mary Tyler on hir former Oath.   E. R. Sec"

The Above is in the Autograph of Gov. Bradftreet and Edward Rawfon.

[50] Son of Governor Simon Bradftreet. In 1698, when the Indians attacked Andover, Bradftreet and his Family were captured; but they were fet at Liberty the fame Day.

tice) that he afflicted the said Dog, and now rid
upon him : He made his Escape into *Pescattequa*-
Government, and the Dog was put to death, and
was all of the Afflicted that suffered death.

[110] At *Andover*, the Afflicted complained of
a Dog, as afflicting of them, and would fall into
their Fits at the Dogs looking upon them ; the
Dog was put to death.

A worthy Gentleman of *Boston*,[51] being about
this time accused by those at *Andover*, he sent by
some particular Friends a Writ to Arrest those
Accusers in a Thousand Pound Action for Defa-
mation, with instructions to them, to inform
themselves of the certainty of the proof, in doing
which their business was perceived, and from
thence forward the Accusations at *Andover* generally ceased.

In *October* some of these Accusers were sent
for to *Gloucester*, and occasioned four Women to
be sent to Prison, but *Salem* Prison being so full
it could receive no more ; two were sent to *Ipswich* Prison.[52] In *November* they were sent for
again by Lieutenant *Stephens*, who was told that
a Sister of his was bewitched ; in their way passing over *Ipswich*-bridge, they met with an old
Woman, and instantly fell into their Fits : But by

---

[51] I am unable to ascertain the
Name of the "worthy Gentleman."
He was doubtless one of those, like
Mr. Calef, not afraid "to take the
Bull by the Horns."

[52] Sarah, the Wife of Peter Cloyce

and Mary Green were probably the
two Persons. The Latter seems to
have made her Escape by the Assistance of John Shepard of Rowley. See Felt, *History of Ipswich
and Hamilton*, 207.

this time the validity of fuch Accufations being much queftioned, they found not that Encouragement they had done elfewhere, and foon withdrew.

Thefe Accufers fwore that they faw three perfons fitting upon Lieutenant *Stephens's* Sifter till fhe died; yet Bond was accepted for thofe Three. And now Nineteen perfons having been hang'd, and one preft to death, and Eight more condemned, in all Twenty and eight, of which above a third part were Members of fome of the Churches in *N. England,* and more than half of them of a good Converfation in general, and not one clear'd. About Fifty having confeft themfelves to be Witches, of which not one Executed; above an Hundred and Fifty in Prifon, and above Two Hundred more accufed. The Special Commiffion of *Oyer* and *Terminer* comes to a period, which has no other foundation than the Governours Commiffion, and had proceeded in the manner of fwearing Witneffes, *viz.* By holding up the hand, (and by receiving Evidences in writing) according to the Ancient Ufuge of this Countrey; as alfo having their Indictments in *Englifh.* In the Tryals, when any were Indicted for Afflicting, Pining, and wafting the Bodies of particular perfons by Witchcraft; it was ufual to hear Evidence of matter foreign, and of perhaps Twenty or Thirty years ftanding, about over-fetting Carts, the death of Cattle, unkindnefs to Relations, or unexpected Accidents befalling after fome quarrel.[53] Whether this was admitted by the Law of *England*, or by what other Law, wants to be determined; the Executions feemed mixt, in prefling to death for not pleading, which moft agrees with the Laws of *England*, and Sentencing Women to be hanged for Witchcraft, according to the former practice of this Country, and not by burning, as is faid to have been the Law of *England*. And though the confefling Witches were many; yet not one of them that confefled their own guilt, and abode by their Confeflion were put to Death.

[111] Here followeth what account fome of thofe miferable Creatures give of their Confeflion under their own hands.

We whofe Names are under written, Inhabitants of Andover, *when as that horrible and tremendous Judgment beginning at* Salem-*Village, in the Year* 1692, (*by fome*) *call'd Witchcraft, firft breaking forth at Mr.* Parris's *Houfe, feveral Young perfons being feemingly afflicted, did accufe feveral perfons for afflicting them, and many there believing it fo to be; we being informed that if a perfon were fick, that the afflicted perfons could tell, what or who was the caufe of that ficknefs.* Jofeph Ballard *of* Andover (*his Wife being fick at the fame time*) *he either from himfelf, or by the advice of others, fetch'd two of the perfons call'd the afflicted perfons, from* Salem-*Village to* Andover : *Which was the*

---

[53] See the Evidence againft Su-fanna Martin, i, Pages 177, *et feq.* See, alfo, Woodward's *Rec. of Salem Witchcraft*, i, 193-206, ii, 215.

beginning of that dreadful Calamity that befel us in Andover. *And the Authority in* Andover, *believing the said Accusations to be true, sent for the said persons to come together to the Meeting-house in* Andover (*the afflicted persons being there.*) *After Mr.* Bernard[54] *had been at Prayer, we were blindfolded, and our hands were laid upon the afflicted persons, they being in their Fits, and falling into their Fits at our coming into their presence (as they said) and some led us and laid our hands upon them, and then they said they were well, and that we were guilty of afflicting of them; whereupon we were all seized as Prisoners, by a Warrant from the Justice of the Peace, and forthwith carried to* Salem. *And by reason of that suddain surprizal, we knowing ourselves altogether Innocent of that Crime, we were all exceedingly astonished and amazed, and consternated and affrighted even out of our Reason; and our nearest and dearest Relations, seeing us in that dreadful condition, and knowing our great danger, apprehending that there was no other way to save our lives, as the case was then circumstantiated but by our confessing ourselves to be such and such persons, as the afflicted represented us to be, they out of tender love and pitty perswaded us to confess what we did confess. And indeed that Confession, that it is said we made, was no other than what was suggested to us by some Gentlemen; they telling us, that we were Witches, and they knew it, and we knew it, and*

---

[54] Mr. John Barnard, who is duly commemorated by Dr. Allen in the *Amer. Biog. Dictionary.* He was Author of several Works.

they knew that we knew it, which made us think that it was so; and our understanding, our reason, and our faculties almost gone; we were not capable of judging our condition; as also the hard measures they used with us, rendred us uncapable of making our Defence; but said any thing and every thing which they desired, and most of what we said, was but in effect a confenting to what they said. Sometime after when we were better composed, they telling of us what we had confessed, we did profess that we were 'Innocent, and Ignorant of such things. And we hearing that Samuel Wardwell *had renounced his Confession, and quickly after Condemned and Executed, some of us were told that we were going after* Wardwell.

Mary Ofgood, Mary Tiler, Deliv. Dane, Abigail Barker, Sarah Wilfon, Hannah Tiler.[55]

[112] It may here be further added concerning thofe that did Confefs, that befides that powerful Argument, of Life (and freedom from hardfhips, and Irons not only promifed, but alfo performed to all that owned their guilt.) There are numerous Inftances, too many to be here inferted, of the tedious Examinations before private perfons, many hours together; they all that time urging them to Confefs (and taking turns to perfwade them) till the accufed were wearied out by being

---

[55] Slight Notices of the Families may be feen in Abbot's *Hiftory of* to which thefe Perfons belonged *Andover.*

forced to ſtand ſo long, or for want of Sleep, &c.
and ſo brought to give an Aſſent to what they
ſaid; they then aſking them, Were you at ſuch a
Witch-meeting, or have you ſigned the Devil's
Book, &c. upon their replying, yes, the whole
was drawn into form as their Confeſſion.

But that which did mightily further ſuch Confeſſions, was their neareſt and deareſt Relations
urging them to it. Theſe ſeeing no other way of
eſcape for them, thought it the beſt advice that
could be given; hence it was that the Huſbands
of ſome, by counſel often urging, and utmoſt ear-
neſtneſs, and Children upon their Knees intreat-
ing, have at length prevailed with them, to ſay
they were guilty.

AS to the manner of Tryals, and the Evidence
taken for Convictions at *Salem*, it is already
ſet forth in Print, by the Reverend Mr. *Cotton
Mather* in his *Wonders of the Inviſible World,* at
the Command of his Excellency Sir *William
Phips;*[56] with not only the Recommendation, but
thanks of the Lieutenant Governour; and with
the Approbation of the Reverend Mr. *J. M.* in
his Poſtſcript to his *Caſes of Conſcience;* which
laſt Book was ſet forth by the conſent of the
Miniſters in and near *Boſton.*[57]

---

[56] It is a Wonder that Mr. Calef did not tell his Readers how
ſhockingly Mr. Mather reported
thoſe Trials; and it is accounted
for only by preſuming that the

Originals were not acceſſible to him,
having been put into the Hands of
Mr. Mather.

[57] Their Names were not printed
according to the original MS. in the

Two of the Judges have alfo given their Sentiments in thefe words, *p.* 147.

The Reverend and worthy Author, having at the direction of his Excellency the Governour, fo far obliged the Publick, as to give fome account of the fufferings, brought upon the Countrey by Witchcrafts, and of the Tryals which have paffed upon feveral executed for the fame.

Upon perufal thereof, We find the matters of Fact and Evidence truly reported, and a profpect given of the Methods of Conviction, ufed in the proceedings of the Court at Salem.

William Stoughton,
Samuel Sewall.

Bofton, October 11, 1692.

And confidering that this may fall into the hands of fuch as never faw thofe Wonders, it may be needful to tranfcribe the whole account he has given thereof, without any variation (but with one of the Indictments annext to the Tryal of each) which is thus prefaced, P. 81, 82, 83.

[113] BUT I fhall no longer detain my Reader from his expected entertainment, in a brief account of the Tryals, which have paffed upon fome of the Malefactors, lately Executed at *Salem*, for the Witchcrafts whereof they ftood

---

Cafes of Confcience. They *are* correctly printed from that MS., however, by the Editor, with fome Re- marks, in his Edition of Mather's *Relation,* xxii. The Order of Subfcription is entirely changed.

convicted. For my own part I was not prefent at any of them; nor ever had I any perfonal prejudice at the perfons thus brought upon the Stage; much lefs, at the furviving Relations of thofe perfons, with and for whom, I would be as hearty a mourner, as any Man living in the World : *The Lord comfort them!* But having received a command fo to do, I can do no other than fhortly relate the chief Matters of Fact, which occurr'd in the Tryals of fome that were Executed; in an Abridgment collected out of the Court-Papers, on this occafion put into my hands. You are to take the truth, juft as it was; and the truth will hurt no good Man. There might have been more of thefe, if my Book would not thereby have been fwelled too big; and if fome other Worthy hands did not perhaps intend fomething further in thefe Collections; for which caufe I have only fingled out four or five, which may ferve to Illuftrate the way of dealing, wherein Witchcrafts ufe to be concerned; and I report matters not as an Advocate, but as an Hiftorian.

They were fome of the Gracious words inferted in the Advice, which many of the Neighbouring Minifters did this Summer humbly lay before our Honourable Judges, We cannot but with all thankfulnefs, acknowledge the fuccefs, which the merciful God has given unto the Sedulous and Affiduous Endeavours of our Honorable Rulers, to detect the Abominable Witchcrafts, which have been committed in the Coun-

try; Humbly praying that the difcovery of thofe
Myfterious, and Mifchievous wickednelfes, may
be perfected. If in the midft of the many Diflatif-
factions among us, the publication of thefe Tryals, may promote fuch a Pious thankfulnefs unto
God, for Juftice being fo far executed among us,
I fhall rejoice that God is glorified; and pray that
no wrong fteps of ours may ever fully any of his
glorious works.

The Indictment of George Burroughs.[58]

Effex ff.   *Anno Regni Regis & Reginæ Williemi & Mariæ, nunc*
              Angliæ, &c. quarto.—

THE Jurors for our Sovereign Lord and Lady
    the. King and Queen prefent, That *George
Burroughs*, late of *Falmouth*, in the Province of
the *Maffachufetts-Bay*, in *New-England*, Clerk.

The 9th Day of *May*, in the fourth Year of the
Reign of our Sovereign Lord and Lady *William*
and *Mary*, by the Grace of God, of *England*,
Scotland, *France* and *Ireland*, King and Queen
Defenders of the [114] Faith, *&c.* And divers
other days and times, as well before as after,
certain deteftable Arts, called Witchcrafts, and
Sorceries, Wickedly and Felonioufly hath ufed,
practifed, and exercifed, at and within the Townfhip of *Salem*, in the County of *Effex* aforefaid,

---

[58] As this Indictment does not appear to be among the Records, its
abfence is accounted for as has been
remarked of other fimilar Documents before noticed; being taken
from the Files and never returned.

in upon, and againft one *Mary Wolcott* of *Salem-*
Village, in the County of *Eſſex*, Single-woman,
by which faid wicked Arts the faid *Mary Wol-*
cott, the Ninth Day of *May*, in the fourth Year
abovefaid, and divers other days and times, as
well before as after, was and is Tortured, Afflicted, Pined, Confumed, Wafted and Tormented,
againft the Peace of our Sovereign Lord and
Lady, the King and Queen, and againft the
Form of the Statute in that Cafe made and provided.

Witneffes, *Mary Wolcott, Sarah Vibber,*[59] *Mercy*
Lewis, Ann Putnam, Eliz. Hubbard.

Endorfed by the Grand Jury, *Billa Vera.* ·

There was alfo a fecond Indictment for afflicting *Elizabeth Hubbard*, the Witneffes to the faid
Indictment were *Elizabeth Hubbard, Mary Wol-*
cott, and *Ann Putnam.*

The third Indictment was for afflicting *Mercy*
Lewis : the Witneffes, the faid *Mercy Lewis,*
Mary Wolcott, Elizabeth Hubbard, and *Ann Put-*
nam.

The fourth for acts of Witchcraft on *Ann Put-*
nam, the Witneffes, the faid *Ann Putnam, Mary*
Wolcott, Elizabeth Hubbard, and *Mary Warren.*[60]

---

[59] This Name as has been mentioned already, is doubtlefs *Bibber*.

[60] Of thefe abandoned Witneffes, we have already had fufficient.

The Tryal of G. B. *as Printed in* Wonders of the
· Invifible World, *from P.* 94 *to* 104.

GLAD fhould I have been, if I had never
known the name of this Man; or never
had this occafion to mention fo much as the firft
Letters of his name. But the Government re-
quiring fome Account of his trial, to be inferted
in this Book, it becomes me with all obedience
to fubmit unto the Order.

1. This *G. B.* was Indicted for Witchcrafts;
and in the Profecution of the Charge againft
him, he was Accufed by five or fix of the Bewitched, as the Author of their Miferies; he was
accufed by Eight of the confeffing Witches, as
being an head Actor at fome of their Hellifh
Randezvouzes, and who had the promife of being
a King in Satan's Kingdom, now going to be
erected; he was accufed by Nine perfons, for
extraordinary lifting, and fuch feats of ftrength
as could not be done without a Diabolical Affiftance. And for other fuch things he was accufed,
until about Thirty Teftimonies[61] were brought

---

[61] About twenty appear in the
Records, which fee, Vol. II, Pages
109, *et feq.* Refpecting Mr. Bur-
rough's great Strength, Samuel Web-
ber, aged about 36, fwore, that
"aboute ceauen or eight Yeares
agoe I liued at Cafco Bay, and
George Burroughs was then Min-
efter there, and haueing heard much
of the great Strength of him fd.
Burroughs; he coming to our Houfe

wee ware in difcourfe aboute the
fame and he then told mee yt he
had put his fingers into the Bung of
a Barrell of Malafes and lifted it
vp and carryed it round him." Salem, Augt. 2d, 1692.

Ann Putnam fwore, that on the
20th of April, 1692, fhe faw the
Apperifbtion of Mr. Burroughs who
tortured her in a terrible Manner;
told her he had had three Wives,

in againft him; nor were thefe judg'd the half of what might have been confider'd for his Conviction: however they were enough to fix the Character of a Witch upon him, according to the Rules of Reafoning, by the judicious *Gaule*, in that cafe directed.

[115] The Court being fenfible, that the Teftimonies of the Parties Bewitched, ufe to have a Room among the Sufpicions, or Prefumptions, brought in againft one Indicted for Witchcraft, there were now heard the Teftimonies of feveral Perfons who were moft notorioufly bewitched, and every day tortured by Invifible hands, and thefe now all charged the Spectres of *G. B.* to

and had bewitched two of them to death; had killed Miftrefs Lawfon becaufe fhe was fo unwilling to go from the Village; had killed Mr. Lawfon's Children becaufe he went to the Eaftward with Sir Edmond [Andros] and preached fo to the Soldiers; had bewitched a great many Soldiers to death when Sir *Edmon* was there, &c. At another time fhe fwore that the two Wives of Mr. Burroughs appeared to her in their Winding-fheets, and told her how they were murdered. Alfo Mrs. Lawfon and her Daughter Ann appeared in the fame Manner; alfo another Woman who told her fhe was Goodman Fuller's firft Wife, and that Mr. Burroughs killed her, becaufe of a Difference between her Hufband and him.

Simon Willard, aged about 42 Years, was at the Houfe of Mr. Robert Lawrence, of Cafco Bay, in Sept., 1689; faw Mr. Burroughs fhow where he took hold of the Gun of about feven foot Barrel, which was behind the Lock; and Mr. B. faid he held it out with one Hand by fo taking it, but the Deponent did not fee him do it. Willard commanded the Fort at Cafco.

Thomas Greenflett, aged about 40 Years, faid he was at Capt. Jofhua Scottow's at Black Point, about the breaking out of the late Indian War, where he faw Mr. B. lift a Gun of fix foot Barrel or thereabout, by putting the Forefinger of his right Hand into the Muzzle; holding it out at Arm's Length. Lieut. Richard Hunnewell and John *Greinflett* being prefent. The above are a few Specimens of the Evidence on which Mr. Burroughs was condemned and executed.

·have a fhare in their Torments. At the Examination of this *G. B.* the bewitched People were
grievoufly harraffed with preternatural Mifchiefs,
which could not poffibly be diffembled ; and they
ftill afcribed it unto the Endeavours of *G. B.* to
kill them. And now upon his Trial, one of the
bewitched perfons teftified, That in her *Agonies*
a little Black-haired Man came to her, faying
his name was *B.* and bidding her fet her hand
unto a Book, which he fhewed unto her ; and
bragging that he was a Conjuror above the ordinary Rank of Witches ; that he often perfecuted
her, with the offer of that Book, faying, fhe
fhould be well, and need fear nobody, if fhe
would but fign it : but he inflicted cruel pains
and hurts upon her, becaufe of her denying fo to
do.[62] The Teftimonies of the other Sufferers,
concurred with thefe ; and it was remarkable,
that whereas Biting, was one of the ways, which
the Witches ufed, for the vexing of the Sufferers,
when they cry'd out of *G. B.* biting them, the
print of his Teeth would be feen on the Flefh
of the Complainers ; and juft fuch a fet of Teeth
as *G. B's.* would then appear upon them, which
could be diftinguifhed from thofe of fome other
Mens.

Others of them teftified, that in their Torments *G. B.* tempted them to go unto a
Sacrament, unto which they perceived him

[62] Several of thofe Girls before mentioned, fwore to about the fame thing.

with a found of Trumpet fummoning of other
Witches; who quickly after the found would
come from all quarters unto the Randezvous.
One of them falling into a kind of Trance, afterwards affirmed, that G. B. had carried her into
a very high Mountain, where he fhewed her
mighty and glorious Kingdoms, and faid he
would give them all to her, if fhe would write
in his Book; but fhe told him, They were none
of his to give; and refufed the Motions; endur-
ing of much mifery for that refufal.[63]

It coft the Court a wonderful deal of trouble
to hear the Teftimonies of the Sufferers; for
when they were going to give in their Depofitions, they would for a long while be taken with
Fits, that made them uncapable of faying any
thing.   The chief Judge afked the Prifoner, who
he thought hindered thefe Witneffes from giving
their Teftimonies? and he anfwered, He fuppofed
it was the Devil.   That Honourable perfon then
replied, How comes the Devil fo loth to have
any Teftimony borne againft you? Which caft
him into very great confufion.[64]

---

[63] The Girl who made oath to
this was Mercy Lewis.   It took
place on the 9th of May, 1692, as
fhe faid: "Mr. Burroughs carried
me up to an exceeding high Mountain and fhewed me all the Kingdoms of the Earth, and told me he
would give them all to me if I would
writ in his Book, and if I would
not, he would thro me down and

break my Neck: but I tould him
they were none of his to give, and
would not writ if he throde me
down on a hundred pichforks."—
Records S. W. ii, 118.

[64] This is only Dr. Mather's
Abridgment of the Record, it will
be remembered.   "Sus. Sheldon
teftifyed that Burroughs two Wives
appeared in their Winding-fheets,

3. It hath been a frequent thing for the bewitched People, to be entertained with Apparitions of Ghofts of murdered People, at the fame
time that the Spectres of the Witches trouble
them. Thefe Ghofts do always [116] affright
the beholders, more than all the other Spectral
Reprefentations; and when they exhibit themfelves, they cry out of being murdered by the
Witchcrafts or other Violences of the perfons
who are then in Spectre prefent. It is further
confiderable, that once or twice thefe Apparitions
have been feen by others, at the very fame time
they have fhown themfelves to the bewitched;
and feldom have there been thefe Apparitions,
but when fomething unufual and fufpected hath
attended the death of the Party thus appearing.
Some that have been accufed by thefe Apparitions, accofting of the bewitched People, who
had never heard a word of any fuch perfons ever
being in the World, have upon a fair Examination, freely and fully confeffed the Murders of
thofe very perfons, although thefe alfo did not
know how the Apparitions had complained of
them. Accordingly feveral of the bewitched
had given in their Teftimony, that they had been
troubled with the Apparitions of two Women,
who faid they were *G. B*'s two Wives; and that
he had been the death of them; and that the

and faid that Man killed them.   knockt down all (or moft) of the
He was bid to look upon Sus.   afflicted who ftood behind him."—
Sheldon. He looked back and   *Ibid.* ii, 109.

Magiſtrates muſt be told of it, before whom, if *B*. upon his Tryal denied it, they did not know but that they ſhould appear again in the Court. Now *G. B.* had been infamous, for the barbarous uſage of his two ſucceſſive Wives, all the Countrey over. Moreover, it was teſtified, the Spectre of *G. B.* threatning of the Sufferers told them he had killed (beſides others) Mrs. *Lawſon* and her Daughter *Ann.* And it was noted, that theſe were the Vertuous Wife and Daughter of one, at whom this *G. B.* might have a prejudice, for being ſerviceable at *Salem*-Village, from whence himſelf had in ill terms removed ſome Years before, and that when they dy'd, which was long ſince, there were ſome odd circumſtances about them, which made ſome of the Attendants there ſuſpect ſomething of Witchcraft, though none imagined from what quarter it ſhould come.

Well *G. B.* being now upon his Tryal, one of the bewitched perſons was caſt into horror at the Ghoſts of *B*'s. two deceaſed Wives, then appearing before him, and crying for vengeance againſt him. Hereupon ſeveral of the bewitched perſons were ſucceſſively called in, who all, not knowing what the former had ſeen and ſaid, concurred in their horror of the Apparition, which they affirmed, that he had before him. But he, though much appalled, utterly denied that he diſcerned any thing of it, nor was it any part of his Conviction.

4. Judicious writers have aſſigned it a great

place, in the Conviction of Witches, when perfons are Impeached by other notorious Witches
to be as ill as themfelves, efpecially if the perfons
have been much noted for neglecting the Worfhip
of God. Now as there might have been Teftimonies enough of *G. B*'s. Antipathy to Prayer,
and the other Ordinances of God, though by his
Profeffion fingularly obliged thereunto; fo there
now came in againft the Prifoner, the Teftimonies of feveral perfons, who [117] confeffed their
own having been horrible Witches, and ever fince
their Confeffions, had been themfelves terribly tortured by the Devils and other Witches, even like
the other Sufferers; and therein undergone the
pains of many deaths for their Confeffions.

Thefe now teftified, that *G. B.* had been at
Witch-meetings with them; and that he was the
perfon who had feduced and compelled them
into the Snares of Witchcraft : that he promifed
them fine Cloaths for doing it; that he brought
Poppets to them, and thorns to ftick into thofe
Poppets, for the afflicting of other People : And
that he exhorted them, with the reft of the Crue
to bewitch all *Salem*-Village; but be fure to do
it gradually; if they would prevail in what they
did.

When the *Lancafhire* Witches were Condemned, I do'nt remember that there was any
confiderable further Evidence, than that of the
bewitched, and than that of fome that had confeffed. We fee fo much already againft *G. B.*

But this being indeed not enough, there were other things to render what had already been produced credible.

5. A famous Divine, recites this among the Convictions of a Witch; the Teftimony of the party bewitched, whether pining or dying; together with the Joint Oaths of fufficient perfons, that have feen certain podigious pranks or feats, wrought by the party accufed. Now God had been pleafed fo to leave this *G. B.* that he had enfnared himfelf, by feveral inftances which he had formerly given of a preternatural ftrength; and which were now produced againft him. He was a very puny Man, yet he had often done things beyond the ftrength of a Giant.[65] A Gun of about 7 Foot barrel, and fo heavy that ftrong Men could not fteadily hold it out, with both hands; there were feveral Teftimonies given in by perfons of Credit and Honor, that he made nothing of taking up fuch a Gun behind the Lock with but one hand, and holding it out like a Piftol, at Arms-end. *G. B.* in his vindication was fo foolifh, as to fay, that an *Indian* was there, and held it out, at the fame time: whereas, none of the Spectators ever faw any fuch *Indian;* but they fuppofed the black Man (as the Witches call the Devil; and they generally fay he refembles an *Indian*) might give him that Affiftance.

[65] By the Teftimony extracted in Note 61, it will be feen that the Doctor's Statement is rather beyond the Record. He may have, and doubtlefs had more than is now extant.

There was Evidence likewife brought in, that he made nothing of taking up whole Barrels fill'd with Mellaffes, or Cyder, in very difadvantageous Poftures, and carrying of them thro' the difficulteft places, out of a Canoa to the Shore.

Yea, there were two Teftimonies, that *G. B.* with only putting the Fore-finger of his right hand into the Muzzel of an heavy Gun, a fowling piece of about fix or feven foot Barrel did lift up the Gun, and hold it out at Arms-end; a Gun which the Deponents, though ftrong men, could not with both hands lift up, and hold out at the Butt-end, as is ufual. Indeed one of thefe Witneffes, was over-perfwaded by fome perfons to [118] be out of way upon *G. B*'s. Tryal; but he came afterwards with forrow for his withdraw, and gave in his Teftimony. Nor were either of thefe Witneffes made ufe of as Evidence in the Tryal.

6. There came in feveral Teftimonies, relating to the Domeftick affairs of *G. B.* which had a very hard Afpect upon him; and not only proved him a very ill Man, but alfo confirmed the belief of the Character, which had been already faftned on him.

'Twas Teftified, that keeping his two fucceffive Wives in a ftrange kind of flavery, he would when he came home from abroad pretend to tell the talk which any had with them. That he has brought them to the point of Death, by his harfh dealings with his Wives, and then made the

People about him to promise that in case Death
should happen they would say nothing of it.
That he used all means to make his Wives Write,
Sign, Seal, and Swear a Covenant never to reveal
any of his Secrets. That his Wives had privately
complained unto the Neighbours about frightly
Apparitions of Evil Spirits, with which their
House was sometimes infested; and that many
such things have been whispered among the
Neighbourhood. There were also some other
Testimonies, relating to the death of People,
whereby the Consciences of an impartial Jury
were convinced, that *G. B.* had bewitched the
persons mention'd in the Complaints. But I am
forced to omit several such Paffages in this as well
as in all the succeeding Tryals, because the Scribes
who took notice of them, have not supplied me.

7. One Mr. *Ruck*, Brother in Law to this *G.
B.* testified that *G. B.* and he himself, and his
Sifter, who was *G. B's.* Wife, going out for two
or three Miles, to gather Strawberries, *Ruck* with
his Sifter, the Wife of G. B. rode home very
softly, with G. B. on foot, in their company, G.
B. stept aside a little into the Bushes, whereupon
they halted and hollow'd for him. He not an-
swering, they went away homewards, with a
quickened pace; without any expectation of seeing him in a confiderable while: and yet when
they were got near home, to their astonishment
they found him on foot, with them, having a
Basket of Strawberries. G. B. immediately then

fell to chiding his Wife, on the account of what she had been speaking to her Brother of him on the Road : which when they wondered at, he said, He knew their thoughts. *Ruck* being startled at that, made some reply, intimating that the Devil himself did not know so far ; but G. B. answered, my god, makes known your thoughts unto me. The Prisoner now at the Bar had nothing to answer unto what was thus witnessed against him, that was worth considering. Only he said, *Ruck* and his Wife left a man with him, when they left him. Which *Ruck* now affirm'd to be false ; and when the Court asked G. B. What the mans name was ? His countenance was much altered ; nor [119] could he say who it was. But the Court began to think that he then stept aside, only that by the Assistance of the black Man, he might put on his invisibility, and in that fascinating Mist, gratify his own jealous humour, to hear what they said of him. Which trick of rendering themselves invisible, our Witches do in their Confessions pretend that they sometimes are masters of ; and it is the more credible, because there is demonstration that they often render many other things utterly invisible.

8. Faultering, Faulty, Unconstant, and contrary Answers upon Judicial and deliberate Examination, are counted some unlucky symptoms of Guilt in all Crimes, especially in Witchcrafts. Now there never was a Prisoner more Eminent for them, than *G. B.* both at his Examination

and on his Tryal. His Tergiverfations, Contradictions, and Falfehoods, were very fenfible: he had little to fay, but that he had heard fome things that he could not prove, Reflecting upon the Reputation of fome of the Witneffes. Only he gave in a Paper to the Jury; wherein, altho' he had many times before granted, not only that there are Witches, but alfo that the prefent Sufferings of the Countrey are the Effects of Horrible Witchcrafts, yet he now goes to evince it, that there neither are nor ever were, Witches, that having made a compact with the Devil, can fend a Devil to torment other People at a diftance. This Paper was tranfcribed out of *Ady;* which the Court prefently knew, as foon as they heard it. But he faid, he had taken none of it out of any Book; for which his evafion afterwards was, that a Gentleman gave him the Difcourfe in a Manufcript, from whence he tranfcribed it.

9. The Jury brought him in Guilty; but when he came to dye, he utterly deny'd the Fact, whereof he had been thus Convicted.[66]

The *Indictment of* Bridget Bifhop.

Anno Regni Regis & Reginæ Willielmi & Mariæ, nunc Angliæ, &c. quarto.

Effex ff. THE jurors for our Sovereign Lord and Lady, the King and Queen prefent, That *Bridget Bifhop,* alias *Oliver,* the Wife of

[66] See Note 153, Page 163, Vol. I.

Edward Bifhop in *Salem,* in the County of *Effex,*
Sawyer, the Nineteenth day of *April,* in the
Fourth Year of the Reign of our Sovereign Lord
and Lady, *William* and *Mary,* by the Grace of
God, of *England, Scotland, France* and *Ireland,*
King and Queen, Defenders of the Faith, &c.
and divers other days.and times, as well before as
after, certain deteftable Arts, called Witchcrafts,
and Sorceries, wickedly and Fellonioufly hath
ufed, practiced, and exercifed at, and within the
Townfhip of *Salem,* in the County of *Effex,* aforefaid, in, upon, and againft one [120] *Mercy Lewis,*
of *Salem*-Village, in the County aforefaid, fingle
Woman; by which faid wicked Arts, the faid
Mercy Lewis, the faid Nineteenth day of *April,*
in the Fourth Year above faid, and divers other
days and times, as well before as after, was and is
Hurt, Tortured, Afflicted, Pined, Confumed,
Wafted and Tormented, againft the Peace of our
Sovereign Lord and Lady, the King and Queen,
and againft the form of the Statute, in that cafe
made and provided.

Endorfed Billa Vera.

Witneffes—*Mary Lewis, Nathaniel Ingarfoll,*
Mr. *Samuel Parris, Thomas Putnam,* Junior, *Mary
Walcott,* Junior, *Ann Putnam,* Junior, *Elizabeth
Hubbard, Abigail Williams.*

There was alfo a Second Indictment, on the
faid *Bifhop,* for afflicting and practifing Witchcraft
on *Abigail Williams.* Witneffes to the faid In-

dictment, were the said *Abigail Williams,* Mr. *Parris, Nathaniel Ingarfoll, Thomas Putnam, Ann Putnam, Mary Walcott, Elizabeth Hubbard.*[67]

The Third Indictment was for afflicting *Mary Walcott,* Witneffes to which said Indictment, were *Mary Walcott, Mercy Lewis,* Mr. *Samuel Parris, Nathaniel Ingarfoll, Thomas Putnam, Ann Putnam, Elizabeth Hubbard, Abigail Williams.*[68]

The Fourth Indictment was for afflicting *Elizabeth Hubbard,* Witneffes to which said Indictment, were the said *Elizabeth Hubbard, Mercy Lewis,* Mr. *Parris, Nathaniel Ingarfoll, Thomas Putnam, Ann Putnam, Mary Walcott, Abigail Williams.*

The Fifth Indictment was for afflicting *Ann Putnam,* Witneffes to which said Indictment, were the said *Ann Putnam,* Mr. *Samuel Parris, Nathaniel Ingarfoll, Thomas Putnam, Mercy Lewis, Mary Walcott, Abigail Williams, Elizabeth Hubbard.*[69]

---

[67] There are four Indictments recorded. The Witneffes to the firft correfpond with the Records. Thofe to the fecond differ by the Omiffion of " John Bligh, and Rebeckah, his Wife; Samuell Shattuck, and Sarah, his Wife; William Bligh, William Stacey; John Loader."

[68] Thefe correfpond with the Original, with fome very flight Difference in the Orthography; and fo of thofe to the fourth Indictment.

[69] It will be feen that much the fame Set of Witneffes figure in moft of the Cafes; and it is furprifing that fuch *ftereotype* Teftimony fhould have been fo long impofed upon the Judges.

The Tryal of Bridget Bifhop, *as printed,
in Wonders of Invifible World,* June 2,
1692. P. 104 to 114.

1. SHE *was Indicted for bewitching feveral perfons in the Neighbourhood.* The Indictment
*being drawn up, according to the form in fuch cafes
ufual, and pleading not guilty, there were brought in
feveral perfons, who had long undergone many kinds
of miferies, which were preternaturally inflicted,
and generally afcribed unto an horrible Witchcraft.
There was little occafion to prove the Witchcraft, it
being evident and notorious to all beholders.* Now
*to fix the Witchcraft on the Prifoner at the Bar,
the firft thing ufed was, the teftimony of the bewitched;
whereof feveral teftified, that the fhape of the* [121]
*Prifoner did oftentimes very grievoufly pinch them,
choak them, bite them, and afflict them; urging them
to write their names in a Book, which the faid Spectre call'd* Ours. *One of them did further teftifie,
that it was the fhape of this Prifoner, with another,
which one day took her from her Wheel, and carrying
her to the River fide, threatned there to drown her,
if fhe did not fign the Book mention'd, which yet fhe
refufed. Others of them did alfo teftifie, that the
faid fhape, did in her threats, brag to them, that fhe
had been the death of fundry perfons, then by her
named. Another teftified, the Apparition of Ghofts
unto the Spectre of* Bifhop, *crying out,* You mur-

dered us. *About the truth whereof, there was in
the matter of Fact, but too much fufpicion.*[70]

2. *It was teftified, that at the Examination of the
Prifoner, before the Magiftrates, the bewitched were
extreamly tortured. If fhe did but caft her Eyes on
them, they were prefently ftruck down; and this in
fuch a manner as there could be no collufion in the
bufinefs. But upon the touch of her hand upon them,
when they lay in their fwoons, they would immediately revive; and not upon the touch of any ones
elfe. Moreover upon fome fpecial Actions of her
Body, as the fhaking of her head, or the turning of
her Eyes, they prefently and painfully fell into the
like poftures. And many of the like accidents now
fell out, while fhe was at the Bar. One at the fame
time teftifying, that fhe faid,* She could not be
troubled to fee the Afflicted thus tormented.[71]

---

[70] The Anfwers of Bridget at
her Examination were Common-
fenfe-like, and carried with them
fuch honeft Simplicity, that it is
Matter of Aftonifhment the Judges
could not diftinguifh between the
moft puerile Abfurdities and Truth.
It appears that fhe had had a Hufband, named Oliver; hence fhe is
often called Bridget Bifhop, alias
Oliver. During her Examination,
the Afflicted apparently fuffered ex-
ceffive Torture. One "Sam. Gold"
afterwards afked her if fhe was not
troubled to fee them fo tormented.
He reported that her Anfwer was
"No. She was not troubled for
them." This was viewed as ftrong
Evidence againft her.

[71] Among all the hard fwearing,
that of "Suf. Sheldon" was perhaps equal to any. She was about
18 Years old. At one Time, June
2d, 1692, fhe faw the "Apperifh-
tion" of Bridget Bifhop, and immediately came two little Children,
Twins, which told her (Bridget) to
her Face that fhe had murdered
them by fetting them into Fits,
whereof they dyed. One John
Cooke, aged 18, fwore about an
Apple which jumped out of his
Hand. John *Blye* and his Wife,
about a Sow of theirs being bewitched, and they "Judged Bifhop
bewitched faid Sow." Elizabeth
Balch of Beverly, aged about 38,
Wife of Benj. B. Jur, "being at

3. *There was Teſtimony likewiſe brought in, that a Man ſtriking once at the place, where a bewitched perſon ſaid, the ſhape of this* Biſhop *ſtood, the bewitched cryed out that he had tore her Coat, in the place then particularly ſpecified; and the Womans Coat was found to be torn in the very place.*[72]

Salem yᵉ very Day that Capt George Corwin was buried, and in yᵉ Euening of ſaid Day coming from ſd. Salem vnto ſd. Beuerly, on Horſeback, with her Siſter, then known by the Name of Abigail Woodburie, now Abigail Waldron lieuing in Wenham, Wife vnto Nathaniell Waldron, riding behinde her; and were come ſo far as Crane Riuer Common ſoe called, Edward Biſhop and his Wife ouertook vs (on horſeback) who are both now in Priſon vnder Suſpition of Witchcraft.'' Bridget complained of her Huſband for riding into the Water, and of riding too faſt. Whereupon an Altercation aroſe, and hard Words were bandied between them. ''And then ſd. Biſhop directed his Speech vnto vs as we rode along, and ſd. that ſhe had been a bad Wife vnto him euer ſince they were marryed, and reckoned vp many of her Miſcarriages towards him; but now of late ſhe was worſe than euer before (and that the ſhe Deuill did come bodyly vnto her, and that ſhe was familiar with the Deuil, and that ſhe ſate vp all ye Night long with yᶜ Deuill) or Words to that Purpoſe. Said Biſhop's Wife made very little Reply.''—*Records S. W.,* i, 167-8.

[72] '' Suſ. Sheldon,'' in additional Teſtimony ſaid, that '' on the fourth Day, at Night, came Goody Olliuer, Mrs. Engliſh, Goodman Corie, and a black Man with a hi crowned hatt, with Books in their Hands. Goody Olliuer bid me touch her Book. I would not ;'' told me ſhe had been a Witch twenty Years. '' Then there came a ſtreacked Snake, creeping ouer her Shoulder, and creep into her Boſom. Mrs. Engliſh had a Yello Bird in her Boſom, and Goodman Corie had two Turcles hang to his Coat, and he opened his Boſom and put his Turcles to his Breſt and gaue them ſuck. Then Goodm. Core and Goody Oliuer kneeled downe before the Black Man and went to prayer. The Black Man told me Goody Olliver had been a Witch 20 years and an half. Then they all ſet to biting mee, and ſo went away. Goodwife Core told me ſhe lived in [B]osſton Priſon. Then ſhe pulled out her breſt and the Black Man gaue her a thing like a blake Pig. It had no Hairs on it. Shee put it to her breſt and gaue it ſuck. Goody Olliver told mee ſhee had killed four Women. Two of them were the Foſters Wifes and John Traskes Wife, and did not

4. *One* Deliverance Hobbs, *who had confeſſed her being a Witch, was now tormented by the Spectres for her Confeſſion. And ſhe now teſtified that this* Biſhop *tempted her to ſign the Book again, and to deny what ſhe had confeſſ'd. She affirmed, that it was the ſhape of this Priſoner, which whipped her with Iron Rods, to compel her thereunto. And ſhe affirmed, that this* Biſhop *was at a General meeting of the Witches in a field, at* Salem-*Village; and there partook of a Diabolical Sacrament, in Bread and Wine then adminiſtered.*[73]

5. *To render it further unqueſtionable, that the Priſoner at the Bar was the Perſon truly charged in this Witchcraft; there was produced many Evidences of other Witchcrafts, by her perpetrated. For inſtance,* John Cook *teſtified, that about five or ſix Years ago, one morning about Sun-Riſe, he was in his Chamber, aſſaulted by the ſhape of this Priſoner: which look'd on him, grinn'd at him, and very much hurt him, with a blow on the ſide of the head; and that on the ſame day about Noon, the ſame ſhape walked in the Room where he was, and an Apple ſtrangely flew out of his hand, into the lap of his Mother, ſix or eight foot from him.*[74]

name the other. Then they did all bite mee."—*Records S. W.* ii, 169-170. Then follows the "Death Warrant" of Bridget Biſhop, dated at Boſton, June the 8th, 1692, ſigned by Lieutenant Governour Stoughton.

[73] Her Teſtimony, as recorded, may be read in the Records as above cited, i, 148-9. It is a Tiſſue of Contradiƈtory Nonſenſe; and if at all relied upon would excite no Wonder, in view of what had gone before.

[74] John Cooke was a young Man of ſome 18 years of Age. It ſhould be remembered that theſe accounts of Evidence are Dr. Mather's Ver-

[122] 6. Samuel Gray, *teftify'd, that about four-teen Years ago, he wak'd on a Night, and faw the Room where he lay full of light ; and that he then faw plainly a Woman between the Cradle and the Bedfide, which looked upon him. He rofe, and it vanifhed; tho he found the Doors all faft : Look-ing out at the Entry door, he faw the fame Woman in the fame garb again, and faid,* In God's name, what do you come for ? *He went to Bed, and had the fame Woman again affaulting him. The Child in the Cradle gave a great Screech, and the Woman difappeared. It was long before the Child could be quieted ; and tho it were a very likely thriving Child, yet from this time it pined away, and after divers Months died in a fad condition. He knew not* Bifhop, *nor her name ; but when he faw her after this, he knew by her countenance, and apparel, and all cir-cumftances, that it was the Apparition of this* Bifhop, *which had thus troubled him.*[75]

7. John Bly *and his Wife, teftified, that he bought a Sow of* Edward Bifhop, *the Hufband of the Pri-foner, and was to pay the price agreed unto another perfon. This Prifoner being angry that fhe was thus hindred from fingring the Money, quarrel'd with* Bly, *foon after which the Sow was taken with ftrange*

fion. He has omitted the moft important Item in Cook's Tefti-mony. He fwore, that after Good-wife Bifhop had ftruck him on the fide of the Head, he faw her go out under the end Window at a little Crevice about as large as one could thruft his hand into. See *Records S. W.* i, 165.

[75] Gray gave his age as about 42 Years. His Teftimony is pretty fully and fairly given above. See *Records, Ibid,* 152-3. He is no-ticed in Savage's *Dictionary,* ii, 299.

Fitts, jumping, leaping, and knocking her head againſt the Fence, ſhe ſeemed blind and deaf, and would neither eat nor be ſucked. Whereupon a Neighbour ſaid, ſhe believed the creature was over-looked; and ſundry other circumſtances concurred, which made the Deponents believe that Biſhop had bewitched it.[76]

8. Richard Coman *teſtified that Eight Years ago, as he lay awake in his Bed, with a light burning in the Room, he was annoyed with the Apparition of this* Biſhop, *and of two more that were ſtrangers to him; who came and oppreſſed him ſo that he could neither ſtir himſelf, nor wake any one elſe: and that he was the Night after moleſted again in the like manner; the ſaid* Biſhop *taking him by the Throat, and pulling him almoſt out of the Bed.* His Kinſman offered for this cauſe to lodge with him; and that night, as they were awake diſcourſing together, this Coman *was once more viſited by the Gueſts which had formerly been ſo troubleſome, his Kinſman being at the ſame time ſtruck ſpeechleſs, and unable to move hand or foot.* He had laid his Sword by him; which thoſe unhappy Spectres, did ſtrive much to wreſt from him, only he held too faſt for them. He then grew able to call the People of his houſe; but altho they heard him, yet they had not power to ſpeak or ſtir, until at laſt, one of the People crying out, *What's the matter!* the Spectres all vaniſhed.[77]

---

[76] This Teſtimony was given June 2d, 1692, The Blighs gave other Teſtimony, alſo, on the ſame Day. John *Blye,* Senior, aged about 57, and William Blye, aged about 15

Years. Theſe teſtified concerning the finding of *Poppitts,* as given in Volume i, Page 173-4.

[77] Coman gave his Age as about 32 years. His Nightmare Story

9. *Samuel Shattuck* teftified, that in the Year, 1680. This *Bridget Bifhop*, often came to his houfe upon fuch frivolous and foolifh Errands, that they fufpected fhe came indeed with a purpofe of Mifchief. Prefently whereupon his Eldeft Child, which was of as promifing health and fenfe, as any Child of its Age, began to droop exceedingly ; and the [123] oftener that *Bifhop* came to the houfe, the worfe grew the Child. As the Child would be ftanding at the Door, he would be thrown and bruifed againft the Stones, by an Invifible hand, and in like fort knock his face againft the fides of the houfe, and bruife it after a miferable manner. Afterwards this *Bifhop* would bring him things to Dye, whereof he could not Imagine any ufe ; and when fhe paid him a piece of Money, the Purfe and Money were unaccountably conveyed out of a lock'd Box, and never feen more. The Child was immediately hereupon taken with terrible Fits, whereof his friends thought he would have died : Indeed he did almoft nothing but cry and fleep, for feveral Months together; and at length his underftanding was utterly taken away. Among other Symptoms of an Inchantment upon him one was, that there was a Board in the garden, whereon he would walk ; and all the Invitations in the world could never fetch him off. About feventeen or eighteen Years after, there came a ftran-

is here a good deal abridged. The curious Reader muft go to the Re- cords, *as publifhed by* Woodward, VoL i, 163-4.

ger to *Shattocks* houfe, who feeing the Child, faid, *This poor Child is bewitched; and you have a Neighbour living not far off who is a Witch.* He added, *Your Neighbour has had a falling out with your Wife ; and fhe faid in her heart, your Wife is a proud Woman, and fhe would bring down her pride in this Child:* He then remembered, that *Bifhop* had parted from his Wife in muttering, and menacing terms, a little before the Child was taken ill. The abovefaid ftranger would needs carry the bewitched Boy with him to *Bifhops* Houfe, on pretence of buying a Pot of Cyder. The Woman entertained him in a furious manner; and flew alfo upon the Boy, fcratching his face till the Blood came, and faying, *Thou Rogue, what? doft thou bring this fellow here to plague me?* Now it feems the Man had faid before he went, that he would fetch Blood of her. Ever after the Boy was followed with grievous Fits, which the Doctors themfelves generally afcribed unto Witchcraft; and wherein he would be thrown ftill into the Fire or Water, if he were not conftantly looked after; and it was verily believed that *Bifhop* was the caufe of it.[78]

10. *John Louder* teftified, that upon fome little controverfie with *Bifhop* about her Fowls, going

---

[78] Shattuck's Teftimony occupies three and an half of Mr. Woodward's quarto Pages. His Age was 41. A part of his Story reminds one of the Man who appeared among his friends with an awfully bruifed Face. On being afked how it happened, replied that the Stones in the Road flew up and ftruck him as he was walking along. Poor Shattuck was unqueftionably injured in the fame way.

well to bed, he did awake in the Night by Moon-
light, and did clearly fee the likenefs of this Woman grievoufly oppreffing him. In which miferable condition fhe held him unable to help
himfelf, till near day. He told *Bifhop* of this;
but fhe utterly denied it, and threatned him very
much. Quickly after this, being at home on a
Lord's Day, with the doors fhut about him, he
faw a black Pig approach him; at which he going to kick, it vanifhed away. Immediately
after fitting down he faw a black thing jump in
at the Window, and come and ftand before him.
The body was like that of a Monkey, the feet
like a Cocks, but the face much like a Mans.
He being fo extremely afrighted, that he could
not fpeak; this Monfter fpoke to him and faid,
I am a Meffenger [124] *fent unto you, for I under-*
ftand that you are in fome trouble of Mind, and if
you will be ruled by me, you fhall want for nothing
in this World. Whereupon he endeavoured to
clap his hands upon it; but he could feel no fubftance, and it jumped out of the Window again;
but immediately came in by the Porch, though
the doors were fhut, and faid, *You had better take*
my counfel! He then ftruck at it with a ftick,
but ftruck only the Groundfel, and broke the
ftick. The Arm with which he ftruck was prefently difenabled, and it vanifhed away. He
prefently went out at the back door, and fpied
this *Bifhop*, in her Orchard, going toward her
Houfe; but he had not power to fet one foot

forward unto her. Whereupon returning into
the Houfe, he was immediately accofted by the
Monfter he had feen before; which Goblin was
now going to fly at him: whereat he cried out,
The whole Armour of God be between me and you!
fo it fprang back, and flew over the Apple-tree;
fhaking many Apples off the Tree in its flying
over. At its leap, it flung dirt with its Feet,
againft the Stomach of the Man; whereon he
was then ftruck dumb, and fo continued for three
Days together. Upon the producing of this
Teftimony, *Bifhop* denied that fhe knew this Deponent. Yet their two Orchards joined, and they
had often had their little quarrels for fome Years
together.[79]

11. *William Stacy* teftified, that receiving Money
of this *Bifhop*, for work done by him, he was gone
but a matter of three Rods from her, and looking
for his Money, found it unaccountably gone from
him. Some time after, *Bifhop* afked him whether his Father would grind her Grift for her?
He demanded why? fhe replied, becaufe folks
count me a Witch. He anfwered, no queftion,
but he will grind it for you; being then gone
about fix Rods from her, with a fmall load in his
Cart, fuddainly the off Wheel flumpt, and funk

<hr>

[79] John Louder gave his Age
"about thirty two." He faid he
lived with Mr. John Gedney in
Salem about feven or eight Years
fince. He was doubtlefs afflicted
by the fame Agents as Samuel Shattuck was, and faw quite as much if
not hurt as much. A black Pig
feemed determined to keep him
Company; but there were fome
other Things equally nondefcript.
See *Records*, i, 160-1.

down into an hole, upon plain ground, ſo that the Deponent, was forced to get help for the recovering of the Wheel. But ſtepping back to look for the hole which might give him this diſaſter, there was none at all to be found. Some time after he was waked in the Night; but it ſeemed as light as day, and he perfectly ſaw the ſhape of this *Biſhop,* in the Room troubling of him, but upon her going out, all was dark again. He charg'd *Biſhop* afterwards with it, and ſhe denied it not; but was very angry. Quickly after, this Deponent having been threatned by *Biſhop,* as he was in a dark Night going to the Barn, he was very ſuddenly taken or lifted from the ground and thrown againſt a Stone-wall; after that he was again hoiſted up, and thrown down a bank, at the end of his Houſe. After this, again paſſing by this *Biſhop,* his Horſe with a ſmall load, ſtriving to draw, all his Gears flew to pieces, and the Cart fell down; and this Deponent going then to lift a bag of Corn, of about two Buſhels, could not budge it with all his might.[80]

[125] Many other pranks of this *Biſhops,* this Deponent was ready to teſtifie. He alſo teſtified, that he verily believed, the ſaid *Biſhop* was the

---

[80] *Stacy* was of Salem, aged thirty ſix, or thereabouts. He goes back fourteen Years, which was the time of the Money Tranſaction. So that Dr. Mather's verſion of the Affair, as though it had juſt happened, is not a fair one. Stacy was often in the ſame Predicament of Shattuck and Louder, only Stone Fences, Stumps and other odd things knocked him about in a manner, which if it ſurpriſed the Magiſtrates, it probably ſurpriſed nobody who might be better acquainted with him. See *Wonders,* Vol. i, 172.

Inftrument of his Daughter *Prifcilla's* death; of which fufpicion, pregnant reafons were affigned.

12. To crown all *John Bly* and *William Bly* teftified, that being employ'd by *Bridget Bifhop*, to help take down the Cellar-wall of the old Houfe, wherein fhe formerly lived, they did in holes of the faid old Wall, find feveral Poppets made up of Rags, and Hogs Briftles, with headlefs Pins in them, the points being outward. Whereof fhe could now give no Account unto the Court, that was reafonable or tolerable.[81]

13. One thing that made againft the Prifoner was, her being evidently convicted of Grofs lying in the Court, feveral times, while fhe was making her Plea. But befides this, a Jury of Women, found a preternatural Tet upon her Body; but upon a fecond fearch, within three or four hours, there was no fuch thing to be feen. There was alfo an Account of other People whom this Woman had Afflicted. And there might have been many more, if they had been enquired for. But there was no need of them.[82]

14. There was one very ftrange thing more, with which the Court was newly entertained. As this Woman was under a guard, paffing by the

---

[81] This Evidence has been referred to in a previous Note.

[82] It was no difficult matter, during a long and tedious Examination, fo to bewilder and confound Perfons of firmer nerves than an aged Matron, and thus make them contradict themfelves, not knowing what to fay and hardly what was faid to them. Refpecting the Jury of Women, who fearched her, the Reader may confult the Records, if his Patience is equal to his Curiofity.

great and fpacious Meeting Houfe of *Salem*, fhe
gave a look towards the Houfe; and immediately
a *Dæmon* invifibly entring the Meeting Houfe,
Tore down a part of it; fo that tho there were
no perfon to be feen there, yet the People at the
Noife running in, found a board which was
ftrongly faftened with feveral Nails, tranfported
unto another quarter of the Houfe.[83]

The Indictment of Sufanna Martin.

Effex ff. *Anno Regni Regis & Reginæ Willielmi & Mariæ, nunc
Angliæ, &c. quarto.*—

THE Jurors for our Soveraign Lord and Lady
the King and Queen, prefent, That *Sufanna
Martin* of *Amefbury* in the County of *Effex*, Wi-
dow, The fecond Day of *May*, in the fourth Year
of the Reign of our Soveraign Lord and Lady
William and *Mary*, by the Grace of God, of
England, Scotland, France and *Ireland,* King and
Queen, Defenders of the faith, &c. And divers
other days and times, as well before as after,
certain deteftable Arts, called Witchcrafts, and
Sorceries, Wickedly and Fellonioufly hath ufed,
practifed, and exercifed, at and within the Townfhip of *Salem*, in the County of *Effex* aforefaid,

[83] It would be much more fatif-
factory if the matter of the Dæmon had been well attefted. If a
Noife, and the Tranfportation of
that Board is all the Evidence that
could be adduced that the Devil
was at work there, it can hardly be
faid to amount to much. Befides,
if the Devil had had any ill will towards the Meeting Houfe, he could
eafily have fet fire to it. His Enmity
to M. Houfes is generally admitted.

M3

in, upon, and againſt one *Mary Wolcott* of *Salem*-Village, in the County of *Eſſex*, Single-Woman, by which ſaid wicked Arts the ſaid *Mary Wolcott*, the Second Day [126] of *May*, in the fourth Year aforeſaid, and at divers other days and times, as well before as after, was and is Tortured, Afflicted, Pined, Conſumed, Waſted and Tormented; as alſo for ſundry other Acts of Witchcraft, by ſaid *Suſanna Martin*, committed and done before and ſince that time, againſt the Peace of our Soveraign Lord and Lady, *William* and *Mary*, King and Queen of *England;* Their Crown and Dignity, and againſt the Form of the Statute, in that Caſe made and provided.

Return'd by the Grand-Jury, *Billa Vera.*

Witneſſes — *Sarah Vibber, Mary Wolcott,* Mr. *Samuel Parris, Elizabeth Hubbard, Mercy Lewis.*

The Sècond Indictment[84] was for afflicting *Mercy Lewis.* Witneſſes—*Samuel Parris, Ann Putnam, Sarah Vibber, Elizabeth Hubbard, Mary Wolcott, Mercy Lewis.*

[84] This ſecond Indictment is given in full in the Records, for which ſee *Records of Salem Witchcraft,* Vol. i, 195-6.

The Trial of *Sufanna Martin, June* 29, 1692. As is Printed, in *Wonders of the Invifible World*, from p. 114 to p. 116.

1. SUSANNA *Martin*, pleading not Guilty, to the Indictment of Witchcrafts brought in againft her; there were produced the Evidences of many persons very fenfibly and · grievoufly bewitched; who all complained of the Prifoner at the Bar, as the perfon whom they believed the caufe of their Miferies.   And now as well as in the other Trials, there was an extraordinary endeavour by Witchcrafts, with cruel and frequent Fits, to hinder the poor Sufferers, from giving in their Complaints; which the Court was forced with much patience to obtain, by much waiting and watching for it.

There was now alfo an Account given, of what had paffed at her firft Examination before the Magiftrates.   The caft of her Eye then ftriking the Afflicted People to the Ground, whether they faw that caft or no : There were thefe among other Paffages between the Magiftrates and the Examinate.

Magiftrate. Pray, what ails thefe People ?

Martin. I don't know.

Magift. But, What do you think ails them ?

Martin. I don't defire to fpend my Judgment upon it.

Magift. Don't you think they are bewitched ?

Martin. No, I do not think they are.

Magift. Tell us your thoughts about them then.

Martin. No, my thoughts are my own when they are in, but when they are out, they are anothers.   Their Mafter—

Magift. Their Mafter;   Who do you think is their Mafter?

Martin. If they be dealing in the black Art, you may know as well as I.

[127] *Magift.* Well, what have you done towards this?

Martin. Nothing at all.

Magift. Why, 'tis you or your appearance.

Martin. I can't help it.

Magift. Is it not your Mafter?   How comes your appearance to hurt thefe?

Martin. How do I know?   He that appeared in the fhape of *Samuel*, a Glorified Saint may appear in any ones fhape.

It was then alfo noted in her, as in others like her, that if the Afflicted went to approach her, they were flung down to the ground.   And, when fhe was afked the reafon of it, fhe faid, I cannot tell, it may be, the Devil bears me more Malice than another.—

The Court accounted themfelves Alarm'd by thefe things, to inquire further into the Converfation of the Prifoner; and fee what there might occur, to render thefe Accufations further credi-

ble.[a] Whereupon *John Allen*, of *Salifbury* teftified, that he refufing, becaufe of the weaknefs of
his Oxen, to Cart fome Staves at the requeft of
this *Martin*, fhe was difpleafed at it, and faid, *It
had been as good that he had; for his Oxen fhould
never do him much more fervice.* Whereupon this
Deponent faid, *Doft thou threaten me, thou old
Witch? I'll throw thee into the Brook:* which to
avoid, fhe flew over the Bridge and efcaped.
But as he was going home, one of his Oxen tired,
fo that he was forced to unyoke him, that he
might get him home. He then put his Oxen
with many more, upon *Salifbury-Beach*, where
Cattle did ufe to get Flefh. In a few Days, all
the Oxen upon the *Beach* were found by their
Tracks, to have run unto the mouth of *Merrimack-River* and not returned; but the next day
they were found come afhore upon *Plum-Ifland.*
They that fought them, ufed all imaginable gen-
tlenefs, but they would ftill run away with a
violence, that feemed wholly Diabolical, till they
came near the mouth of *Merrimack-River;* when
they ran right into the Sea, fwimming as far as
they could be feen. One of them then fwam
back again, with a fwiftnefs amazing to the beholders, who ftood ready to receive them, and
help up his tired Carcafs: but the Beaft ran furioufly up into the Ifland, and from thence thorough
the Marifhes, up into *Newbury* Town, and fo up

---

[a] The Above is but a very fmall   by the Records. See *Wonders of*
Part of the Examination, as appears   *the Invifible World*, Vol. I, P. 175.

into the Woods; and there after a while found near
Ameſbury. So that of Fourteen good Oxen,
there was only this ſaved: the reſt were all caſt
up, ſome in one place, and ſome in another,
Drowned.[85]

4. *John Atkinſon* teſtified, that he exchanged a
Cow, with a Son of *Suſanna Martins,* whereat
ſhe muttered, and was unwilling he ſhould have
it. Going to receive this Cow, tho he Ham-
ſtring'd her, and halter'd her, ſhe of a tame Creature grew ſo mad, that they could ſcarce get her
along. She broke all the Ropes that were faſt-
ened unto her, and tho ſhe was tied [128] faſt
unto a Tree, yet ſhe made her eſcape, and gave
them ſuch further trouble, as they could aſcribe
to no cauſe but Witchcraft.[86]

5. *Bernard Peache* teſtified that being in Bed,
on a Lords Day Night, he heard a ſcrabbling at
the Window, whereat he then ſaw *Suſanna Martin*
come in, and jump down upon the floor. She
took hold of this Deponents Feet, and drawing
his body up into an heap, ſhe lay upon him near
two hours; in all which time he could neither
ſpeak nor ſtir. At length when he could begin
to move he laid hold on her hand, and pulling it
up to his mouth, he bit three of her Fingers as
he judged to the Bone. Whereupon ſhe went

---

[85] Lieut. John Allen was of Saliſbury; and his Age 45. The Accuſed troubled him at ſome previous
Period, but the Time he does not
ſtate.

[86] The Witneſs, John Atkinſon,
was aged about 56 Years. His
Evidence related to Matters of ſome
five Years paſt. See *Wonders of
Inviſible World,* Vol. I, Page 178.

from the Chamber down the Stairs, out at the door. This Deponent thereupon called unto the people of the Houfe to advife them of what paffed; and he himfelf did follow her. The People faw her not; but there being a Bucket at the Left hand of the door, there was a drop of Blood on it; and feveral more drops of Blood upon the Snow, newly fallen abroad. There was likewife the print of her 'two Feet, juft without the Threfhold; but no more fign of any footing further off.[87]

At another time this Deponent was defired by the Prifoner, to come unto a hufking of Corn, at her Houfe; and fhe faid, *If he did not come, it were better that he did!* He went not; but the night following, *Sufanna Martin,* as he judged, and another came towards him. One of them faid, *here he is!* but he, having a Quarterftaff, made a blow at them. The Roof of the Barn broke his blow; but following them to the Window, he made another blow at them, and ftruck them down; yet they got up, and got out, and he faw no more of them.

About this time, there was a Rumour about the Town, that *Martin* had a broken head; but the Deponent could fay nothing to that.

The faid *Peache* alfo teftified, the bewitching of Cattle to Death, upon *Martin's* difcontents.

---

[87] Peache's Evidence was of Troubles of about ten Years before. He faid his Age was about 42; and at the Time of the Witchcraft complained of, he lived with William Ofgood, of Salifbury.

6. *Robert Downer* teſtified, that this Priſoner being ſome years ago proſecuted at Court for a Witch, he then ſaid unto her, *He believed ſhe was a Witch.* Whereat ſhe being diſatisfied, ſaid, *That ſome ſhe Devil would ſhortly fetch him away;* which words were heard by others, as well as himſelf; the night following, as he lay in his Bed, there came in at the Window, the likeneſs of a Cat, which flew upon him, and took faſt hold of his Throat, lay on him a conſiderable while, and almoſt killed him; at length he remembered what *Suſanna Martin* had threatened the Day before, and with much ſtriving, he cried out, *Avoid thou the Devil, In the name of God the Father, the Son, and the Holy Ghoſt, avoid:* Whereupon it left him, leaped on the Floor, and flew out at the Window.

And there alſo came in ſeveral Teſtimonies that before ever *Downer* ſpoke a word of this Accident, *Suſanna Martin* and her Family had related how this *Downer* had been handled.[88]

[129] 7. *John Kembal* teſtified, that *Suſanna Martin,* upon a cauſeleſs diſguſt had threatned him about a certain Cow of his, that ſhe ſhould never do him any more good, and it came to paſs accordingly; for ſoon after the Cow was found ſtark dead on the dry ground, without any Diſtemper to be diſcerned upon her. Upon which he was followed with a ſtrange death upon

---

[88] Downer's Age was 52, and he belonged to Saliſbury. What he ſwore to was of Events which happened "ſeveral Years ago."

more of his Cattle. Whereof he loft in one Spring, to the value of 30 *l.* But the faid *John Kembal,* had a further Teftimony to give in againft the Prifoner, which was truly admirable. Being defirous to furnifh himfelf with a Dog, he applied himfelf to buy one of this *Martin,* who had a Bitch with Whelps in her Houfe, but fhe not letting him have his choice; he faid, *He would fupply himfelf then at one* Blezdels. Having mark'd a Puppy which he liked at *Blezdels,* he met George Martin, the Hufband of the Prifoner going by, who afked whether he would not have one of his Wives Puppy's ; and he anfwered, No. The fame Day one *Edmund Eliot,*[89] being at *Martins* Houfe heard *George Martin* relate where this *Kembal* had been, and what he had faid ; whereupon *Sufanna Martin* reply'd, *If I live I'll give him Puppies enough.* Within a few days after this, *Kembal* coming out of the Woods, there arofe a little black Cloud in the *N. W.* and *Kembal* immediately felt a force upon him, which made him not able to avoid running upon the ftumps of Trees that were before him, albeit he had a broad plain cart way before him ; but tho he had his Axe alfo on his Shoulder to endanger him in his falls, he could not forbear going out of his way to tumble over them. When he came below the Meeting-Houfe, there appeared unto him

[89] Three Perfons of the Name of *Eliot* are implicated in the Witch Court Proceedings—Andrew, Daniel, and this Edmund, who was of Amefbury. The Bofton *Eliots* were of this Lineage.

a little thing like a Puppy of a darkifh Colour, and it fhot backwards and forwards between his Legs. He had the Courage to ufe all poffible endeavours of cutting it with his Axe, but he could not hit it; the Puppy gave a jump from him and went, as to him it feem'd into the Ground. Going a little further there appeared unto him a black Puppy, fomewhat bigger than the Firft, but as black as a Coal. It's motions were quicker than thofe of his Axe. It flew at his Belly, and away at his Throat, fo over his Shoulders one way, and then over his Shoulders another way, his heart now began to fail him, and he thought the Dog would have tore his Throat out. But he recovered himfelf, and called upon God in his diftrefs, and naming the name of Jefus Chrift it vanifhed away at once. The Deponent fpoke not one word of thefe Accidents, for fear of affrighting his Wife. But the next morning, *Edmund Eliot* going into *Martins* houfe, this Woman afked him, where *Kembal* was? He replied, at home a Bed, for ought he knew. She returned; they fay he was frighted laft night. *Eliot* afked with what? She anfwered with Puppies. *Eliot* afked, where fhe heard of it, for he had heard nothing of it! She rejoined, about the Town. Altho' *Kembal* had mentioned the matter to no creature living.[90]

[90] John Kimball was of Amef-bury, and was "aged 45 or vp-ward." His fwearing was to Oc-currencies of twenty-three Years ftanding; that about that Time he removed from Newbury to Amef-bury, having bought Piece of Land of Geo. Martin. The Tef-timony of Kimball occupies three and an half Pages of the *Records,* i, 218-21. He probably married Mary Hobbs, in Newbury.

[130] 8. *William Brown* teftified, that Heaven having blefſ'd him with a moſt Pious and Prudent Wife, this Wife of his, one day met with *Sufanna Martin:* but when ſhe approached juſt unto her, *Martin* vaniſhed out of fight, and left her extreamly affrighted. After which time the faid *Martin* often appeared unto her, giving her no little trouble; and when ſhe did come, ſhe was vifited with Birds that forely peck'd and prick'd her; and fometimes a bunch like a Pullets Egg would rife on her Throat, ready to choak her, till ſhe cry'd out, *Witch, you ſhan't choak me!* While this good Woman was in this Extremity, the Church appointed a Day of Prayer on her be-half; whereupon the trouble ceaſ'd; ſhe faw not *Martin* as formerly; and the Church inſtead of their Faſt, gave thanks for her deliverance. But a confiderable while after, ſhe being fummoned to give in fome Evidence at the Court, againſt this *Martin*, quickly this *Martin* came behind her, while ſhe was Milking her Cow, and faid unto her, *For thy defaming me at Court, I'll make thee the miſerableſt Creature in the World.* Soon after which ſhe fell into a ſtrange kind of Dif-temper, and became horribly Frantick, and un-capable of any Reafonable Action, the Phyficians declaring, that her Diſtemper was preternatural, and that fome Devil had certainly bewitched her; and in that condition ſhe now remained.[91]

[91] This Teſtimony was by Wil-liam Browne, of Amefbury, whofe Age was 70 Years. or "ther about." What he fwore to happened, he

9. *Sarah Atkinfon* teftified, that *Sufanna Martin* came from *Amefbury*, to their Houfe at *Newbury*, in an extraordinary Seafon, when it was not fit for any one to Travel. She came (as fhe faid unto *Atkinfon*) all that long way on foot. She bragg'd and fhow'd how dry fhe was; nor could it be perceived that fo much as the Soles of her Shoes were wet. *Atkinfon* was amazed at it, and profeffed, that fhe fhould herfelf have been wet up to the Knees, if fhe had then come fo far; but *Martin* reply'd, *She fcorned to be drabbled!* It was noted that this Teftimony upon her Tryal, caft her into a very fingular confufion.[92]

10. *John Preffy* teftified, that being one Evening very unaccountably bewildred near a Field of *Martin*, and feveral times as one under an Enchantment, returning to the place he had left, at length he faw a Marvellous light, about the bignefs of an half Bufhel, near two Rood out of the way. He went and ftruck at it with a Stick, and laid it on with all his might. He gave it near Forty blows; and felt it a palpable fubftance.

faid "about on or to and thirty Years ago." The Trouble feems to have been between Mrs. Martin, and Browne's Wife, who was afflicted with hyfteric Fits: infomuch that fhe was infane. He had applied to Doctors Fuller and Crofby, but they faid her Complaint was fupernatural, and that fome evil Perfon had bewitched her. When in this State fhe would not own him for her Hufband, and "afked him whether he did not mett with one Mr. Bent of Abey in England by whom he was divorced."—*Records S. W.*, i, 206-8.

[92] Sarah Atkinfon was probably the Wife of John Atkinfon, mentioned at Note 86. The "fingular Confufion" appears to have been gratuitoufly thrown in by Dr. Mather. It is not in the Record. Her Age is given as 48 Years, or thereabouts.

But going from it, his heels were ftruck up, and he was laid with his back on the ground; fliding as he thought into a Pit: from whence he recovered, by taking hold on the Bufh; altho afterwards he could find no fuch Pit in the place. Having after his recovery, gone five or fix Rood, he faw *Sufanna Martin* ftanding on his Left hand, as the Light had done before; but they changed no words with one another. He could fcarce find his Houfe in his return; but at length he got home, extreamly af[131]frighted. The next Day it was upon enquiry underftood, that *Martin* was in a miferable condition by pains and hurts that were upon her.

It was further teftified by this Deponent, that after he had given in fome Evidence againft *Sufanna Martin* many Years ago, fhe gave him foul words about it, and faid, *He fhould never profper, more particularly, that he fhould never have more than two Cows: that tho he were never fo likely to have more, yet he fhould never have them.* And that from that very day to this; namely for Twenty Years together, he could never exceed that number; but fome ftrange thing or other ftill prevented his having of any more.[93]

11. *Jarvis Ring* teftified that about Seven Years ago he was oftentimes grievoufly oppreffed in the

---

[93] John Preffy, aged 53, and "Marah his Wif aged 46 or ther abouts." It comes out in this Evidence, but is not mentioned by Mather, that at fome 20 Years previous, this John Preffy and Wife had teftified againft Mrs. Martin, and that fhe had accufed them of taking a falfe Oath. Such was the Origin of much of the Teftimony.

Night; but faw not who troubled him, until at
laft he lying perfectly awake, plainly faw *Sufanna
Martin* approach him. She came to him and
forcibly bit him by the Finger; fo that the print
of the bite is now fo long after to be feen upon
him.

12. But befides all thefe Evidences, there was
a moft wonderful Account of one *Jofeph Ring*
produced on this occafion. This Man has been
ftrangely carried about by *Dæmons.* From one
Witch-meeting to another, for near two Years
together; and for one quarter of this time they
made him and kept him Dumb, though he is
now again able to fpeak. There was one *T. H.*[94]
who having, as 'tis judged, a defign of Engaging·
this *Jofeph Ring* in a fnare of Devilifm, contrived
a while, to bring this *Ring* two Shillings in Debt
unto him. Afterwards this poor Man would be
vifited with unknown fhapes, and this *T. H.*
fometimes among them; which would force him
away with them, unto unknown places, where he
faw Meetings, Feaftings, Dancings; and after his
return wherein they hurried him along thro the
Air, he gave demonftrations to the Neighbours,
that he had indeed been fo tranfported. When
he was brought unto thefe hellifh meetings, one
of the firft things they ftill did unto him, was to
give him a knock on the back, whereupon he
was ever as if bound with Chains, uncapable of

[94] Thomas Hardy of Great Ifland,   ceals his Name, except by the Ini-
at Pafcatequay. Why Mather con-   tials, is not known.

ftirring out of the place, till they fhould releafe him. He related, that there often came to him a Man, who prefented him a Book, whereto he would have him fet his hand; promifing to him that he fhould then have even what he would; and prefenting him with all the delectable things, perfons, and places, that he could imagine. But he refufing to fubfcribe, the bufinefs would end with dreadful fhapes, noifes and fcreeches, which almoft fcared him out of his wits. Once with a Book, there was a Pen offer'd him, and an Ink-horn, with liquor in it, that feem'd like Blood: but he never touched it.[95]

This Man did now affirm, that he faw the Prifoner at feveral of thofe hellifh Randezvouzes.

[132] *Note* — This Woman was one of the moft Impudent, Scurrilous, wicked Creature in the World; and fhe did now throughout her whole Tryal, difcover herfelf to be fuch an one. Yet when fhe was afked what fhe had to fay for herfelf, her chief plea was, that fhe had led a moft vertuous and holy life.

[95] Jarvis Ring's Cafe could have been nothing but one of Nightmare. Jofeph Ring, brother of Jarvis, was 27 years of Age. They belonged to Salifbury. His Evidence compares very well with that of the Girls and other Mifcreants, foregone. The Teftimonies of the Amefbury Accufers were taken before "Robert Pike, *Affift.*"

The Indictment of *Elizabeth How.*

Essex ss.   *Anno Regni Regis & Reginæ Williemi & Mariæ, nunc Angliæ, &c. quarto.*——

THE Jurors for our Soveraign Lord and Lady, the King and Queen prefent, That *Elizabeth How,* Wife of *James How* of *Ipswich,* the Thirty firft Day of *May,* in the Fourth Year of the Reign of our Soveraign Lord and Lady, *William* and *Mary,* by the Grace of God, of *England, Scotland, France,* and *Ireland,* King and Queen, Defenders of the Faith, *&c.* and divers other days and times, as well before as after, certain deteftable Arts, called Witchcrafts and Sorceries, wickedly and Fellonioufly hath ufed, practiced, and exercifed at, and within the Townfhip of *Salem,* in the County of *Effex* aforefaid, in, upon, and againft one *Mary Wolcott,* of *Salem*-Village, in the County aforefaid, fingle Woman; by which faid wicked Arts, the faid *Mary Wolcott,* the faid Thirty firft Day of *May,* in the Fourth Year as abovefaid, and divers other days and times, as well before as after, was and is Tortured, Afflicted, Pined, Confumed, Wafted and Tormented; and alfo for fundry other Acts of Witchcrafts, by faid *Elizabeth How;* committed and done before and fince that time, againft the Peace of our Sovereign Lord and Lady, the King and Queen, and againft the form of the Statue, in that cafe made and provided.

Witnesses — *Mary Wolcott, Ann Putnam, Abigail Williams, Samuel Pearly,* and his Wife *Ruth, Joseph Andrews,* and Wife *Sarah, John Sherrin, Joseph Safford, Francis Lane, Lydia Foster, Isaac Cummins,* Junior.

There was also a second Indictment for afflicting of *Mercy Lewis.*

Witnesses — *Mercy Lewis,. Mary Wolcott, Abigail Williams, Ann Putnam, Samuel Pearly* and Wife, *Joseph Andrews* and Wife, *John Sherrin, Joseph Safford, Francis Lane, Lydia Foster.*

[133] The Tryal of *Elizabeth How,*⁹⁶ *June* 30, 1692. As is Printed In *Wonders of the Invisible World,* from P. 126 to P. 132, inclusively.

1. ELIZABETH *How,* pleading, not Guilty to the Indictment of Witchcrafts, then charged upon her; the Court, according to the usual proceeding of the Courts in *England;* in such Cases, began with hearing the Deposition of several Afflicted People, who were grievously tormented by sensible and evident Witchcrafts,

---

⁹⁶ The Indictment does not appear in the Records, probably for the Reason that it had been given to or taken by Dr. Mather, and never returned. Mrs. How was of Topsfield, Wife of James How of that Town. Ephraim Wildes was the Constable who apprehended her. Her Examination was on the 30th of May, 1692, occupies two Pages, and was taken down by Mr. "Sam. Parris."

and all complained of the Prifoner, as the caufe
of their trouble. It was alfo found that the
Suffers were not able to bear her look, as likewife, that in their greateft fwoons, they diftinguifhed her touch from other Peoples, being
thereby raifed out of them.

And there was other Teftimony of People to
whom the fhape of this *How*, gave trouble Nine
or Ten Years ago.[97]

2. It has been a moft ufual thing for the bewitched perfons at the fame time that the Spectres reprefenting the Witches, Troubled them to
be vifited with Apparitions of Ghofts, pretending
to have been murdered by the Witches then rep-
refented.   And fometimes the confeffions of the
Witches afterwards acknowledged thofe very
Murders, which thefe Apparitions charged upon
them; altho they had never heard what Information had been given by the Sufferers.

There was fuch Apparitions of Ghofts teftified
by fome of the prefent Sufferers, and the Ghofts
affirmed that this *How* had murdered them:
which things were fear'd, but not proved.[98]

[97] The Author has not taken up
the refpective Parties who gave Evidence.   Among others, no Notice
is taken of that of two Minifters,
namely, Mr. Samuel Phillips and
Mr. Edward Payfon, both of Rowley.   Mr. Phillips gave his Age as
about 67.   Mr. *Paifon* did not
ftate his.   Their Teftimonies were
paffed over undoubtedly becaufe

they did not in the leaft criminate
Mrs. How; nor did they pretend
that they had feen any Thing like
Witchcraft.

[98] They were not only not proved,
but there are no Teftimonies recorded containing thefe Ghoft Stories.   The following Witneffes are
not noticed by Dr. Mather, viz.:
Samuel Perley, aged about 52, and

3. This *How* had made fome attempts of Joining to the Church at *Ipfwich*, feveral Years ago; but fhe was denied an Admiffion into that holy Society, partly thro a fufpicion of Witchcraft, then urged againft her. And there now came in Teftimony of preternatural Mifchiefs, prefently befalling fome that had been Inftrumental to debar her from the Communion whereupon fhe was intruding.[99]

his Wife about 46. Deborah Hadley, aged about 70 Years; had lived near Elizabeth How ("ye Wife of James How, Jr. of Ipfwich 24 year.") She gave her a good Character. Mrs. Hadley teftified on the 24th of June. The next Day Daniel Warner, Sen. gave in his Teftimony. It was of the fame tenor of Mrs. Hadley's. John Warner, Sen[r]. alfo figned the fame Evidence. They had been well acquainted with Mrs. How "aboue 20 yeers." So Simon Chapman and his Wife teftified. Simon gave his Age as about 48 — "hath ben acquainted with the Wiuef of James How, iun[r]. as a Naybar for this 9 or 10 Yers;" never knew any harm of her, and "found hur jouft in hur delling, faythfooll," &c.

[99] Againft fuch gratuitous, and to fay the leaft, hearfay Teftimony, the Doctor fhould, in fairnefs, have noticed fuch Evidence as that referred to in the laft Note. A few others muft not be overlooked. Jofeph Knowlton ftated that he had been acquainted with Mrs. How, as a Neighbor, and fometimes boarded in the Houfe at his firft coming to live in thefe Parts, which was about ten Years ago. He and his Wife Mary both gave her a good Character. His Age was "forty tu," and his Wife's "thurty-tu."

James How, Sen., aged about 94, teftified that he had lived by Elizabeth, the Wife of James How, Jun[r], for about thirty Years; and, "fetting a fide humain Infurmity," fhe always behaved well, becoming her Place as a Daughter and Wife in all Relations.

Refpecting the Church Difficulty, referred to in the Text, one Jacob Fofter, aged about 29, fwore, that "fome Years agoe," as Goodwife How was about to join the Church, his Father was a Means of preventing it. Whereupon his Mare was loft for feveral Days. When found fhe looked as if fhe had been miferably beaten and abufed. Sworn June 30th, 1692. Thomas Andrews of Boxford, aged about 50, told a more ridiculous Story about a Mare, belonging to Jofiah Comings, Sen[r] of Topsfield.

4. There was a particular Depofition of *Jofeph Safford*, that his Wife had conceived an extream Averfion, to this *How*, on the reports of her Witchcrafts; but *How* one day taking her by the hand, and faying, *I believe you are not Ignorant of the great fcandal, that I lye under, by an Evil report raifed upon me.* She immediately, unreafonably, and unperfwadeably, even like one Inchanted, began to take this Womans part. *How* being foon after propounded, as defiring an Admiffion to the Table of the Lord, fome of the Pious Brethren were unfatisfied about her. The Elders appointed a meeting to hear matters objected againft her; and no arguments in the World could hinder this Goodwife *Safford* from going to the Lecture. She did indeed promife with much ado that fhe would not go to the Church-meeting; yet fhe could not refrain going thither alfo. [134] *How's* affairs there were fo canvaffed, that fhe came off rather Guilty, than cleared; neverthelefs Goodwife *Safford* could not forbear taking her by the Hand, and faying, *Tho you are condemned before Men, you are juftified before God.* She was quickly taken in a very ftrange manner; Frantick, Raving, Raging, and crying out, *Goody* How *muft come into the Church; fhe is a precious Saint, and tho' fhe be condemned before Men, fhe is juftified before God.* So fhe continued for the fpace of two or three hours; and then fell into a Trance. But coming to herfelf, fhe cried out, *Ha! I was miftaken!* afterwards again repeated,

Ha! I was miſtaken! being aſked by a ſtander by, Wherein ? ſhe replied, *I thought Goody* How *had been a precious Saint of God, but now I ſee ſhe is a Witch: ſhe has bewitched me and my Child, and we ſhall never be well, till there be Teſtimony for her, that ſhe may be taken into the Church.*[100]

And *How* ſaid afterwards, *That ſhe was very ſorry to ſee* Safford *at the Church-meeting mentioned.* Safford *after this, declared herſelf to be Afflicted by the ſhape of* How, *and from that ſhape ſhe endured many miſeries.*

5. *John How*, Brother to the Huſband of the Priſoner teſtified that he refuſing to accompany the Priſoner unto her Examination as was by her deſired, immediately ſome of his Cattle, were bewitched to Death, leaping Three or four Foot high, turning about, ſqueaking, falling and dying at once; and going to cut off an Ear, for an uſe, that might as well perhaps have been omitted, the Hand wherein he held his Knife was taken very Numb; and ſo it remained, and full of pain for ſeveral Days; being not well at this very time. And he ſuſpected this Priſoner, for the Author of it.[101]

6. *Nehemiah Abbot* teſtified, that unuſual and miſchievous accidents would befall his Cattle, whenever he had any difference with this Priſoner.

---

[100] Joſeph Safford gave his Age about 60.

[101] John How gave his Age as about 50. The Doctor has made ſome wretched Miſtakes in his Abſtract of this Teſtimony. It was his Sow that "leaped up about three or foure foot hie," and fell down dead. The *ſqueaking* belonged to the Swine, and not to the Cattle.

Once particularly fhe wifhed his Ox choaked, and within a little while, that Ox was choaked with a Turnip in his Throat. At another time, refufing to lend his Horfe, at the requeft of her Daughter, the Horfe was in a preternatural manner abufed. And feveral other odd things of that kind were teftified.[102]

7. There came in Teftimony that one Goodwife *Sherwin,* upon fome difference with *How* was bewitched, and, that fhe died, charging this *How* of having an hand in her Death. And that other People had their Barrels of Drink unaccountably mifchiev'd, fpoiled, and fpilt upon their difpleafing her.[103] •

The things in themfelves were trivial; but there being fuch a courfe of them, it made them the more to be confidered. Among others, *Martha Wood* gave her teftimony, that a little after, her Father had been employed in gathering an account of this *How's* Converfation, they once and again loft great quantities of Drink, out of their Veffels, in fuch a [135] manner, as they could afcribe to nothing but Witchcraft. As alfo that *How* giving her fome Apples, when fhe had eaten of them, fhe was taken with a very ftrange kind of a maze, infomuch that fhe knew not what fhe faid or did.[104]

---

[102] I do not find any Note of Nehemiah Abbot's Evidence in the Records.

[103] This has reference, perhaps, to the Ghoft Stories darkly hinted at by the Dr. Mather in a previous Page.

[104] I have not noticed Martha Wood's Evidence among the Records. The "great Quantities of Drink" reported loft, was probably found by fome of the Witneffes already noticed.

8. There was likewife a Clufter of Depofitions, that one *Ifaac Cummings*, refufing to lend his Mare, unto the Hufband of this *How;* the Mare was within a Day or two taken in a ftrange condition. The beaft feemed much abufed; being bruifed, as if fhe had been running over the Rocks, and marked where the Bridle went, as if burnt with a red hot Bridle. Moreover one ufing a Pipe of Tobacco for the cure of the Beaft, a blew flame iffued out of her, took hold of her hair, and not only fpread and burnt on her, but it alfo flew upwards towards the Roof of the Barn, and had like to have fet the Barn on fire. And the Mare dy'd very fuddenly.[105]

9. *Timothy Perly* and his Wife, teftified, not only that unaccountable Mifchiefs befel their Cattle, upon their having of differences with this Prifoner; but alfo that they had a Daughter deftroyed by Witchcrafts; which Daughter ftill charged *How*, as the caufe of her Affliction; and it was noted that fhe would be ftruck down, whenever *How* were fpoken of. She was often endeavoured to be thrown into the Fire, and into the Water, in her ftrange Fitts; tho her Father had corrected, for charging *How* with bewitching her, yet (as was teftified by others alfo) fhe faid fhe was fure of it, and muft dye ftanding to it. Accordingly fhe charged *How* to the very death;

---

[105] Cummin's Teftimony occupies above two folid Pages. His Age was about fixty Years. His Chriftian Name was miftaken by Mather, being Ifaac inftead of Jofiah, as appears by the Records.

and faid, *Tho* How *could Afflict and Torment her Body, yet fhe could not hurt her Soul, and that the truth of this matter would appear when fhe fhould be dead and gone.*[106]

10. *Francis Lane* teftified, that being hired by the Hufband of this *How* to get him a parcel of Pofts and Rails, this *Lane* hired *John Pearly* to affift him. This Prifoner then told *Lane* that fhe believed the Pofts and Rails would not do, becaufe *John Pearly* helped him; but that if he had got them alone without *John Pearly's* help, they might have done well enough. When *James How* came to receive his Pofts and Rails of *Lane,* *How* taking them up by the Ends, they, tho good and found yet unaccountably broke off, fo that *Lane* was forced to get Thirty or Forty more. And this Prifoner being informed of it, fhe faid, *She told him fo before : becaufe* Pearly *helped about them.*[107]

11. Afterwards there came in the Confeffions of feveral other (penitent) Witches, which affirmed this *How* to be one of thofe who with them had been baptized by the Devil in the River, at *Newberry-Falls :* before which he made them there

---

[106] Timothy *Perley* and his Wife Deborah teftified, June 1ft, 1692, that he was about 39 Years of Age, and his Wife about 33. The Abftract above is exceedingly defective. See the *Records,* ii, 73-4.

[107] Francis Lane gave his Age as about 27, and faid that the Time the Witches afflicted the Rails was about "feauen" Years ago, and makes a long Story out of it; but it is of a Piece with moft of the Evidence. Lane's Parentage has not been traced.   •

kneel down by the Brink of the River, and Worſhip him.[108]

[136] *The Indictment of* Martha Carryer.[109]

Eſſex ſſ. *Anno Regni Regis & Reginæ Wilielmi & Mariæ, nunc Angliæ, &c. quarto.—*

THE Jurors for our Soveraign Lord and Lady the King and Queen, preſent, That *Martha Carryer*, Wife of *Thomas Carryer* of *Andover*, in the County of *Eſſex*, Huſbandman, The Thirty firſt Day of *May*, in the fourth Year of the Reign of our Soveraign Lord and Lady *William* and *Mary*, by the Grace of God, of *England, Scotland, France* and *Ireland*, King and Queen, Defenders of the Faith, *&c.* And divers other days and times, as well before as after, certain deteſtable Arts, called Witchcrafts, and Sorceries, Wickedly and Fellouniouſly hath uſed, practiſed, and exerciſed, at and within the Townſhip of *Salem*, in

[108] They affirmed that many of thoſe wretched Souls had been Baptized at Newberry Falls; and at ſeveral other Rivers and Ponds; and as to the Manner of Adminiſtration, the Great Officer of *Hell* took them up by the Body, and putting their Heads into the Water, ſaid over them, *Thou art mine, and I have full Power over the:* And thereupon they engaged and covenanted to renounce GOD, CHRIST, their *ſacred Baptiſm*, and the whole Way of *Goſpel Sal-* vation; and to uſe their utmoſt Endeavours to oppoſe the Kingdom of CHRIST, and to ſet up and *advocate* the Kingdom of *Satan.—* Lawſon, *Second Edition*, 118. See, alſo, Vol. I, Page 102-3.

[109] Complaint was made againſt Martha Carrier on the 28th of May, by Joſeph Houlton and John Wallcott, both of Salem. John Ballard, Conſtable, arreſted her. John *Bayley*, Aſſiſtant Conſtable of Andover, ſummoned the Witneſſes. See *Records* S. *W.* ii, 54, 55, &c.

the County of *Essex* aforesaid, in, upon, and
against one *Mary Wolcott* of *Salem*-Village, Single
Woman, in the County of *Essex* aforesaid; by
which said wicked Arts the said *Mary Wolcott,*
the Thirty first Day of *May,* in the fourth Year
aforesaid, and at divers other days and times, as
well before as after, was and is Tortured, Afflicted, Pined, Consumed, Wasted and Tormented;
against the Peace of our Soveraign Lord and Lady,
William and *Mary,* King and Queen of *England;*
their Crown and Dignity, and against the Form
of the Statute, in that Case made and provided.

Witnesses — *Mary Wolcott, Elizabeth Hubbard,
Ann Putnam.*

There was also a Second Indictment for afflicting *Elizabeth Hubbard,* by Witchcraft. Witnesses — *Elizabeth Hubbard, Mary Wolcott, Ann
Putnam, Mary Warrin.*

The Trial of *Martha Carryer,* August 2,
1692. As may be seen in *Wonders of
the Invisible World,* from P. 132, to
138.

1. **M**Artha Carryer was indicted for the bewitching of certain persons according to
the form usual in such Cases: Pleading not Guilty
to her Indictment; there were first brought in a
considerable number of the Bewitched persons;

who not only made the Court fenfible of an horrid Witchcraft committed upon them, but alfo depofed, That it was *Martha Carryer*, or her fhape, that grievoufly tormented them by biting, pricking, pinching and choaking them. It was further depofed that while this *Carryer* was on her Examination before the Magiftrates, the poor People were fo tortured, that every one expected their Death upon the very fpot; but that upon the binding of *Carryer* they were eafed. [137] Moreover the looks of *Carryer* then laid the Afflicted People for dead, and her Touch, if her Eyes at the fame time were off them, raifed them again. Which things were alfo now feen upon her Tryal. And it was teftified, that upon the mention of fome having their Necks twifted almoft round by the fhape of this *Carryer*, fhe replied, *Its no matter, tho their Necks had been twifted quite off.*[110]

2. Before the Tryal of this Prifoner, feveral of her own Children had frankly and fully confeffed not only that they were Witches themfelves, but that this their Mother had made them fo. This confeffion they made with great fhows of Repentance, and with much Demonftration of Truth. They related Place, Time, Occafion; they gave an Account of Journeys, Meetings, and Mifchiefs by them performed; and were very credi-

---

[110] Martha Carrier underwent the ufual Examination, which occupies two Pages, and the Original is in the Hand of Mr. Samuel Parris. The above is but a very unfatisfactory Abridgement of it.

ble in what they faid. Neverthelefs, this Evidence
was not produced againft the Prifoner at the Bar,
in as much as there was other Evidence enough
to proceed upon.[111]

3. *Benj. Abbot* gave in his Teftimony, That laft
March was a Twelve month, this *Carryer* was
very angry with him, upon laying out fome Land
near her Hufbands.   Her expreffions in this
Anger were, *That fhe would ftick as clofe to* Abbot,
*as the Bark ftuck to the Tree; and that he fhould
repent of it afore feven Years came to an end, fo as
Doctor* Prefcot *fhould never cure him.*   Thefe
words were heard by others, befides *Abbot* himfelf, who alfo heard her fay, *She would hold his
Nofe as clofe to the Grind-ftone as ever it was held
fince his name was* Abbot.   Prefently after this he
was taken with a fwelling in his Foot, and then
with a Pain in his Side, and exceedingly tormented.   It bred unto a Sore, which was lanced
by Dr. *Prefcot,* and feveral Gallons of Corruption ran out of it.   For fix Weeks it continued
very bad; and then another Sore bred in his
Groin, which was alfo lanced by Dr. *Prefcot.*
Another Sore bred in his Groin which was likewife Cut, and put him to very great mifery.   He

---

[111] It appears from Lawfon's Account that fuch Accufations were
much heeded.   He fays—"Several
have confeffed againft their own
Mothers, that they were Inftru-
ments to bring them into the *Devil's Covenant,* to the undoing of their
Body and Soul.   And fome Girls
of Eight or Nine Years of Age did
declare that after they were fo be-
trayed by their Mothers, to the
Power of *Satan,* they faw the *Devil*
go in their *own fhapes* to afflict others."—Page 118-19.

was brought unto Death's door, and fo remained until *Carryer* was taken and carried away by the Conftable. From which very day he began to mend, and fo grew better every day, and is well ever fince.[112]

Sarah Abbot alfo his Wife teftified, that her Hufband was not only all this while Afflicted in his Body; but alfo that ftrange, extraordinary and unaccountable calamities befel his Cattle; their Death being fuch as they could guefs at no Natural Reafon for.[113]

4. *Allin Toothaker* teftified, that *Richard* the Son of *Martha Carryer*, having fome difference with him, pull'd him down by the Hair of the Head, when he rofe again, he was going to ftrike at *Richard Carryer*, but fell down flat on his back to the ground, and had not power to ftir Hand or foot, until he told *Carryer* he yielded; and then he faw the fhape of *Martha Carryer*, go off his Breaft.

[138] This *Toothaker* had received a wound in the Wars, and he now teftified, that *Martha Carryer* told him, *He fhall never be cured.* Juft afore the apprehending of *Carryer*, he could thruft a Knitting-Needle into his wound four Inches deep, but prefently after her being feized, he was thoroughly healed.

He further teftified, that when *Carryer* and he fometimes were at variance, fhe would clap her

---

[112] Benjamin Abbot was of Andover, and his Age was about 31.   [113] Sarah Abbot gave her Age as about 32 Years.

Hands at him and fay, *He fhould get nothing by it.*
Whereupon he feveral times loft his Cattle, by
ftrange Deaths, whereof no natural caufes could
be given.[114]

5. *John Roger* alfo teftified, that upon the
threatning words of this malicious *Carryer*, his
Cattle would be ftrangely bewitched; as was
more particularly then defcribed.[115]

6. *Samuel Prefton* teftified, that about two Years
ago, having fome difference with *Martha Carryer*,
he loft a Cow in a ftrange, preternatural, unufual
manner; and about a Month after this, the faid
Carryer, having again fome difference with him,
fhe told him, *He had lately loft a Cow, and it fhould
not be long before he loft another!* which accordingly came to pafs; for he had a thriving and
well kept Cow, which without any known caufe
quickly fell down and died.[116]

7. *Phebe Chandler* teftified, that about a Fort-
night before the Apprehenfion of *Martha Carryer*, on a Lords Day, while the Pfalm was finging
in the Church, this *Carryer* then took her by the

---

[114] Allen Toothaker was a young Man, aged about 22 Years. He may have received his Wound when the Indians attacked An-dover, as mentioned in an earlier Note.

[115] John *Rogers* was of Billerica. He gave his Age as about 50. His Teftimony takes up a quarto Page in the Records. Three Years later, viz., Auguft 5th, 1695, he, with feveral others, was killed at Biller-ica by the Indians.

[116] Samuel Prefton gave his Age as about 41 Years. He fwore he "loft a Cow in a ftrange Manner." That *ftrange Manner*, it is evident from his Story, referred to the Way in which fhe was caft, and not being able to free herfelf, died. The *preternatural* and *unufual* being thrown in by the Doctor.

Shoulder, and fhaking her, afked her, *Where fhe lived?* fhe made her no Anfwer, altho as *Carryer,* who lived next door to her Father's Houfe, could not in Reafon but know who fhe was. Quickly after this, as fhe was at feveral times croffing the Fields fhe heard a Voice that fhe took to be *Martha Carryers,* and it feem'd as if it were over her head. The Voice told her, *She fhould within two or three Days be Poifon'd:* Accordingly within fuch a little time, one half of her Right Hand became greatly fwollen and very painful; as alfo part of her Face; whereof fhe can give no Account how it came. It continued very bad for fome days; and feveral times fince fhe has had a great pain in her Breaft; and been fo feized on her Legs that fhe has hardly been able to go. She added that lately, going well to the Houfe of God, *Richard* the Son of *Martha Carryer,* look'd very earneftly upon her, and immediately her Hand which had formerly been Poifoned, as is abovefaid, began to pain her greatly, and fhe had a ftrange burning at her Stomach; but was then ftruck deaf, fo that fhe could not hear any of the Prayer, or Singing, till the two or three laft words of the Pfalm.[117]

8. One *Fofter,* who confeffed her own fhare in the Witchcraft, for which the Prifoner ftood In-

---

[117] It is only neceffary to ftate that Phebe Chandler was but about 12 Years old, as a Reafon that no Notice fhould be taken of her Evidence; and notwithftanding near two folid Pages of her Teftimony are in the Records. However, Bridget Chandler, her Mother, aged 40 Years, corroborated the Daughter's Story.

dicted, affirmed, that fhe had feen the Prifoner at fome of their Witch-meetings, and that it was this *Carryer*, who perfwaded her to be a Witch. She confeffed that the Devil carried them on [139] a Pole to a Witch-meeting, but the Pole broke, and fhe hanging about *Carryer's* Neck, they both fell down, and fhe then received an hurt by the fall, whereof fhe was not at this very time recovered.[118]

9. One *Lacy*, who likewife confeffed her fhare in this Witchcraft, now teftified that fhe and the Prifoner, were once bodily prefent, at a Witch-meeting in *Salem*-Village, and that fhe knew the Prifoner to be a Witch, and to have been at a Diabolical Sacrament, and that the Prifoner was the undoing of her and her Children, by enticing them into the Snare of the Devil.[119]

10. Another *Lacy*, who alfo confeffed her fhare in this Witchcraft, now teftified that the Prifoner was at the Witch meeting in *Salem*-Village, where they had Bread and Wine adminiftred unto them.

11. In the time of this Prifoners Tryal, one *Sufanna Shelden*[120] in open Court, had her Hands unaccountably tied together, with a Wheel-band, fo faft, that without cutting, it could not be loofed. It was done by a Spectre; and the Sufferer affirm'd, it was the Prifoners.

[118] This has reference to Ann Fofter, of Salem Village. See *Records S. W.*, ii, 136-7.

[119] Mary Lacy was Wife of Lawrence Lacy, of Andover, and Daughter of Ann Fofter. See *Ibid.*, ii, 139-40. This "other Lacy" was alfo named "Mary." *Ibid.*, 142.

[120] Sufanna Sheldon was a ready Witnefs in a large Number of Cafes, as has already been noticed.

Memorandum. This *Rampant Hag, Martha Carryer*, was the perfon of whom the Confeſſions of the Witches and of her own Children, among the reſt, agreed, that the Devil had promiſed her, ſhe ſhould be Queen of Hell.[121]

Thus far the Account given in *Wonders of the Inviſible World;* in which ſetting aſide ſuch words as theſe, in the Tryal of *G. B.* viz. [*They* (i. e.) *the Witneſſes were enough to fix the character of a Witch upon him.*]

In the Tryal of *Biſhop*, theſe words, [*but there was no need of them*] i. e. of further Teſtimony.

In the Tryal of *How*, where it is ſaid, [and there came in Teſtimony of preternatural Miſchiefs, preſently befalling ſome that had been inſtrumental to debar her from the Communion,

---

[121] No Teſtimony appears to have been omitted that could be tortured by any Conſtruction againſt "this rampant Hag," by the Author, while all that went to clear her was rejected. Fortunately the Caſe is changed, and the whole is ſpread before diſintereſted Inquirers, or enough upon which to form a correct Judgment. Mr. Francis Dane, the ſecond Miniſter of Andover, dared to give his Thoughts upon the Witchcraft Caſes. Theſe he communicated to the Court, and the Scribe recorded them among the Evidence. He ſaid he had lived above forty Years in Andover, and in his "healthfull Yeares had been frequent among yᵉ Inhabitants in their Habitations," and never heard of anything of the Nature of Witchcraft until the Arreſts the laſt Summer (1692). If there were any Suſpicions that Martha Carrier was a Witch, before ſhe was apprehended, he ſaid he had never heard of it; and "as for any other Perſons, I had no Suſpicion of them, and had Charity been put on, the Diuel would not have had ſuch an Advantage againſt us, and I beleeve many innocent Perſons have been accuſed." This Teſtimony of an aged and worthy Gentleman (then 77), well acquainted with all the Circumſtances, and with the Accuſed, ſhould accompany that againſt "the rampant Hag."

whereupon fhe was *intruding.*] *Martin* is call'd [one of the moft impudent, fcurrilous, wicked Creatures in the World.] In his Account of *Martha Carryer*, he is pleafed to call her [a *Rampant Hag,*] &c.

Thefe Expreffions as they manifeft, that he wrote more like an Advocate than an Hiftorian; fo alfo that thofe that were his Imployers were not miftaken in their choice of him for that work, however he may have mift it in other things.

As in his owning (in the Tryal of *G. B.*) That the *Teftimony of the bewitched, and confeffors was not enough againft the Accufed,* for it is known that not only in *New-England,* fuch Evidence has been taken for fufficient, but alfo in *England,* as himfelf there owns, and will alfo hold true of *Scotland, &c.* they having proceeded upon fuch Evidence, to the taking away of the Lives of many, to affert that this is not enough, is to tell the World that fuch Executions were but fo many Bloody Murders; which furely was not his intent to fay.[122]

[140] His telling that the Court began to think

---

[122] This Paffage caufed Dr. Mather to utter fome very wrathful Expreffions againft the Author. He fays, or rather, his Defenders for him: "What was done in the dark Time of our Troubles from the *Invifible World,* all honeft Men believe, they did in Confcience of the *Oath* of God upon them, and they followed unto the beft of their Underftanding, as we are informed, the Precedents of *England* and *Scotland,* and *other Nations* on fuch a dark and doleful Occafion. When they found the Matter carried beyond the Reach of Mortals, they ftopt."—*Some Few Remarks,* 6; *Magnalia,* B. ii, 64.

that *Burroughs* ftept afide to put on Invifibility, is a rendring them fo mean Philosophers, and fuch weak Chriftians, as to be fit to be impofed upon by any filly pretender.

His calling the Evidence againft *How* trivial, and others againft *Burroughs*, he accounts no part of his Conviction ; and that of lifting a Gun with one Finger, its being not made ufe of as Evidence, renders the whole but the more per-plext. (Not to mention the many miftakes therein contain'd.)

Yet all this (and more that might have been hinted at) does not hinder, but that his Account of the manner of Trials of thofe for Witchcraft is as faithfully related as any Tryals of that kind, that was ever yet made publick ; and it may alfo be reafonably thought that there was as careful a Scrutiny, and as unqeftion'd Evidences improved, as had been formerly ufed in the Tryals of oth-ers, for fuch crimes in other places.[123]   Tho in-deed a fecond part might be very ufeful to fet forth which was the Evidence Convictive in thefe Tryals, for it is not fuppofed, that Roman-tick or Ridiculous ftories fhould have any influ-ence, fuch as biting a Spectres Finger fo that the Blood flowed out, or fuch as *Shattock's* Story of 12 Years ftanding, which yet was prefently 18 Years or more, and yet a Man of that excellent Memory, as to be able to recall a fmall difference

[123] See Volume I, Pages 35, 86.

his Wife had with another Woman when Eighten Years were paft.

As it is not to be fuppofed that fuch as thefe could Influence any Judge or Jury, fo not unkindnefs to relations, or God's having given to one Man more ftrength than to fome others, the over-fetting of Carts, or the death of Cattle, nor yet Excrefcencies (call'd Tets) nor little bits of Rags tied together (call'd Poppets.)   Much lefs any perfons illnefs, or having their Cloaths rent when a Spectre has been well hanged, much lefs the burning the Mares Fart, mentioned in the Tryal of *How.*

None of thefe being in the leaft capable of proving the Indictment; The fuppofed Criminals were Indicted for Afflicting, *&c.* fuch and fuch particular perfons by Witchcraft, to which none of thefe Evidences have one word to fay, and the Afflicted and Confeffors being declared not enough, the matter needs yet further explaining.

But to proceed, the General Court having fat and enacted Laws, particularly one againft Witchcraft, affigning the Penalty of Death to any that fhall feed, reward or employ, *&c.* Evil Spirits, though it has not yet been explained what is intended thereby, or what it is to feed, reward or imploy Devils, *&c.* yet fome of the Legiflators have given this inftead of an Explanation, that they had therein but Copied the Law of another Country.[124]

January 3. By vertue of an Act of the General Court, the firſt Superior Court was held at *Salem*, for the County of *Eſſex*, the Judges appointed were Mr. *William Stoughton* (the Lieutenant Governor) *Thomas* [141] *Danforth, John Richards, Wait Winthorp*, and *Samuel Sewall*, Eſquires. Where Ignoramus was found upon the ſeveral Bills of Indictment againſt Thirty, and *Billa-Vera* againſt Twenty ſix more ; of all theſe Three only were found Guilty by the Jewry upon Trial, two of which were (as appears by their Behaviour) the moſt ſenſeleſs and Ignorant Creatures that could be found ; beſides which it does not appear what came in againſt thoſe more than againſt the reſt that were acquitted.[125]

The Third was the Wife of *Wardwell*, who was one of the Twenty Executed, and it ſeems they had both confeſſed themſelves Guilty ; but he retracting his ſaid Confeſſion, was tried and Executed ; it is ſuppoſed that this Woman fearing her Huſbands fate, was not ſo ſtiff in her denials of her former Confeſſion, ſuch as it was. Theſe Three received Sentence of Death.[126]

---

[124] What the Laws of England were on the Subject of Witchcraft has been exhibited in the Introduction to the firſt Volume. Their Abrogation by Parliament, through the exertions of Lord Talbot, took place in 1736. See Douglaſs' *Summary*, i, 451.

[125] I do not find the Court Proceedings at this Period.

[126] The Indictments and Examination of Samuel Wardwell may be ſeen in the Records, in the uſual Form. He was of Andover, and is ſtyled Carpenter. His firſt Indictment was for afflicting one

At theſe Tryals ſome of the Jewry made In-
quiry of the Court, what Account they ought to
make of the Spectre Evidence? and received for
Anſwer [as much as of Chips in Wort][127]
January 31, 169⅔. The Superior Court began
at *Charleſtown*, for the County of *Middleſex*, Mr.
Stoughton, M. *Danforth*, M. *Winthorp*, and Mr.
Sewall Judges, where ſeveral had Ignoramus re-
turned upon their Bills of Indictment, and *Billa
Vera* upon others.[128]

Martha Sprague of Boxford, in
Auguſt laſt (1692). The ſecond
charges, that "about 20 Yeares
agoe, in the Towne of Andivor,
he the ſaid Samuel Wardell, with
the Evill Speritt the Devill [did
felloniouſly make] a Couenant
wherein he promiſed to honor,
worſhip and belieue the Devill
Contrary to the Stattute." His
Examination was before John Hig-
ginſon, Esq. on Sept. 1ſt, 1692.
He was then about 46 Years old.
His ſtrange Anſwers clearly indi-
cate a ſtate of Inſanity. Martha
Sprague, aged 16, ſwore to being
bewitched by him. Ephraim Foſ-
ter of Andover, aged about 34,
ſwore that he foretold Events by
looking in people's Hands; "would
eaſt his Eyes down upon yᵉ ground
allways before he told enything."
Thomas Chandler, aged about 65,
often heard ſaid Wardell tell
young Perſons their Fortunes. Joſeph Ballard, aged about 41, ſwore
that his Brother John Ballard told
him that Samuel Wardell told

him, that he (Wardell) had bewitched his (Joſeph Ballard's) Wife.
Abigail Martin of Andover, aged
16, ſaid that ſome time laſt Winter
S. Wardell and John *Farnam* were
at her Fathers. W. told F.'s Fortune. He alſo told Jeams Bridge's
Fortune. See *Records S. W.* ii,
146-153.

[127] *Q. D. of no Account whatever.* I do not find that the Expoun-
ders of Proverbs have fallen upon
this.

[128] One of the Original *Billa veras*
is now before me, and runs thus:
"The Depoſition of Mercy Lewis
Aged [19.] This Deponent teſtifieth
and ſaith that laſt Night Philip Engliſh and his Wife came to mee, alſo
Goodwife Daſten, Eliza Johnſon,
and Old Pharoh of Linn: ſd. Mrs.
Engliſh vrged mee to ſet my Hand
to a Booke, and told mee ſhe would
afflict me dreadfully and kill me if
I did not: Said alſo if I would but
touch the Booke I ſhould bee well,
or elſe I ſhould never. Mrs. Engliſh ſaid ſhe might bring the Book

In the time the Court ſat, word was brought
in, that a Reprieve was ſent to *Salem*, and had
prevented the Execution of Seven of thoſe that
were there Condemned, which ſo moved the
chief Judge, that he ſaid to this effect, *We were
in a way to have cleared the Land of theſe, &c. who
it is obſtructs the courſe of Juſtice I know not ; the
Lord be merciful to the Countrey*, and ſo went off
the Bench, and came no more that Court :[129] The
moſt remarkable of the Tryals, was of *Sarah
Daſton*, ſhe was a Woman of about 70 or 80
Years of Age, To uſher in her Tryal, a report
went before, that if there were a Witch in the
World ſhe was one, as having been ſo accounted
of, for 20 or 30 Years ; which drew many People
from *Boſton, &c.* to hear her Tryal.   There were
a multitude of Witneſſes produced againſt her ;
but what Teſtimony they gave in ſeemed wholly
forreign, as of accidents, illneſs, &c. befalling
them, or theirs after ſome Quarrel ; what theſe
teſtified was much of it of Actions ſaid to be
done 20 Years before that time.   The Spectre-
Evidence was not made uſe of in theſe Tryals, ſo
that the Jewry ſoon brought her in not Guilty,

now ſhe thought everie one of them
would bee cleared, and now at this
preſent Time before the Grandiury
ſd Philip Engliſh, his Wife, and old
Pharoh, come into the Roome, or
their Shape and ſtroke mee on the
Breſt, and almoſt choaked mee, and
ſaid they would ſtrangle me if they
could.   *Owned before the Grand-*

*iury upon the Oath ſhe had taken,
Janr* 12*th*, 169⅔. *Atteſts* Robert
Payne, *Foreman.*"   All in the Autograph of Mr. Saml. Parris, except
the Signature of Payne.   See Appendix, Number III.

[129] The " Chief Judge," it will
be remembered, was Lieut. Gov.
Stoughton.

her Daughter and Grand-daughter, and the reſt
that were then tried, were alſo acquitted. After
ſhe was cleared Judge *Danforth* Admoniſhed her
in theſe words, *Woman, Woman, repent, there are
ſhrewd things come in againſt you;* ſhe was re-
manded to Priſon for her Fees, and there in a
ſhort time expired.[130] One of *Boſton* that had
been at the Tryal of *Daſton*, being the ſame Evening in company with one of the Judges [142] in
a publick place, acquainted him that ſome that
had been both at the Tryals at *Salem* and at this
at *Charleſtown*, had aſſerted that there was more
Evidence againſt the ſaid *Daſton* than againſt any
at *Salem*, to which the ſaid Judge conceeded,
ſaying, *That it was ſo.* It was replied by that
perſon, *that he dare give it under his hand, that
there was not enough come in againſt her to bear a
juſt reproof.*

April 25, 1693. The firſt Superior Court was
held at *Boſton*, for the County of *Suffolk*, the
Judges were the Lieutenant Governour, Mr. *Danforth*, Mr. *Richards*, and Mr. *Sewall*, Eſquires.

Where (beſides the acquitting Mr. *John Aldin*
by Proclamation) the moſt remarkable was, what
related to *Mary Watkins*, who had been a Servant,

---

130 The Complainants were "Mr.
Thomas Putnam, and Mr. John Putnam, Jr., of Salem Village." She
is ſtyled ſingle Woman, "of Red-
ding," and her Name is ſpelt Duf-
ting, Daſtin, and Daſting, in the
Records. It would be intereſting
to know if ſhe was a Relative of

the noted Heroine, Hannah Duſtin,
of Haverhill, who ſlew her Indian
Captors, and eſcaped out of Captivity in 1697. Mr. Chaſe, the
able Hiſtorian of Haverhill, does
not ſeem to have conſulted the Records at Salem, as we find nothing
of this Caſe in his Hiſtory.

and lived about Seven Miles from *Boſton*, having formerly Accuſed her Miſtreſs of Witchcraft, and was ſuppoſed to be diſtracted, ſhe was threatned if ſhe perſiſted in ſuch Accuſations to be puniſhed, this with the neceſſary care to recover her Health, had that good effect, that ſhe not only had her Health reſtored, but alſo wholly acquitted her Miſtreſs of any ſuch Crimes, and continued in Health till the return of the Year, and then again falling into Melancholy humours ſhe was found ſtrangling herſelf; her Life being hereby prolonged, ſhe immediately accuſed herſelf of being a Witch; was carried before a Magiſtrate and committed. At this Court a Bill of Indictment was brought to the Grand Jury againſt her, and her confeſſion upon her Examination given in as Evidence, but theſe not wholly ſatisfied herewith, ſent for her, who gave ſuch account of herſelf, that they (after they had returned into the Court to aſk ſome Queſtions) Twelve of them agreed to find Ignoramus, but the Court was pleaſed to ſend them out again, who again at coming in returned it as before.

She was continued for ſome time in Priſon, *&c.* and at length was ſold to *Virginia.* About this time the Priſoners in all the Priſons were releaſed.

To omit here the mentioning of ſeveral Wenches in *Boſton, &c.* who pretended to be Afflicted, and accuſed ſeveral, the Miniſters often viſiting them, and praying with them, concerning whoſe Affliction Narratives are in being. In Manufcript not only thefe, but the generality of thofe Accufers may have fince convinc'd the Minifters by their vicious courfes that they might err in extending too much Charity to them.

The conclufion of the whole in the *Maffachufetts* Colony was Sir *William Phips*, Governour, being call'd home, before he went he pardon'd fuch as had been condemned, for which they gave about 30 Shillings each to the Kings Attorney.[131]

In *Auguft* 1697. The Superior Court fat at *Hartford*, in the Colony of *Connecticut*, where one Miftrefs *Benom* was tried for Witchcraft, fhe [143] had been accufed by fome Children that pretented to the Spectral fight; they fearched her feveral times for Tets; they tried the Experiment of cafting her into the Water, and after this fhe was Excommunicated by the Minifter of *Wallinsford*. Upon her Tryal nothing material appeared againft her, fave Spectre Evidence, fhe was acquitted, as alfo her Daughter, a Girl of Twelve or Thirteen Years old, who had been likewife Accufed; but upon renewed Complaints againft them, they both flew into *New-York* Government.[132]

---

131 If this was fuppofed to be dealing juftly by the Accufed, the Government Officers of that Day muft have had a very *angular* Idea of Juftice, as underftood by upright Men of the prefent Day. Such a Courfe reminds one of "Lidford Law," and of thofe fen-

tenced "to be hanged and to pay 40 fhillings."

132 "One that many Years fince was Executed at Hartford, in Connecticut Colony, on the Account of Witchcraft, confeffed, that fhe had employed Evil Spirits to be revenged on feveral; but that when

Before this the Government Iſſued forth the following Proclamation.

*By the Honourable the Lieutenant Govern-
our, Council and Aſſembly of his Majeſties*[133] *Province of the* Maſſachuſetts Bay,
in General Court Aſſembled.

Whereas the Anger of God is not yet turned away, but his Hand is ſtill ſtretched out againſt his People in manifold Judgments, particularly in drawing out to ſuch a length the troubles of *Europe*,[134] by a perplexing War; and more eſpecially, reſpecting ourſelves in this Province, in that God is pleaſed ſtill to go on in diminiſhing our Subſtance, cutting ſhort our Harveſt, blaſting our moſt promiſſing undertakings more ways than one, unſettling of us, and by his more Immediate hand, ſnatching away many out

---

ſhe would have had them do the Like to Mr. Stone (the Eminent Teacher of the Church there) they told her, they had not leave to do it: Nor is this to be Evaded by ſaying ſome Perſons (as of late in New England) have falſely accuſed themſelves, for this Perſon was upon Rational Grounds, thought to be a true Penitent, before her Death. We cannot argue, that becauſe ſome have failed in their curſed Attempts, that therefore never any Succeeded.

But the known Succeſs of many was that which emboldened others to Endeavour the Like.".—I. Mather, in *Angelographia, To the Reader.* See, alſo, *Remarkable Providences* (by the ſame), Chap. V.

[133] William III, Mary being dead. She died on the 28th Dec., 1694. Was Dau. of James II, by A. Hyde.

[134] The "perplexing war" of this Period is ſketched with a Maſter's Hand by Macaulay in his *Hiſtory of England.*

of our Embraces, by ſudden and violent Deaths,
even at this time when the Sword is devouring
ſo many both at home and abroad, and that after
many days of publick and Solemn addreſſing of
him. And altho conſidering the many Sins prevailing in the midſt of us, we cannot but wonder
at the Patience and Mercy moderating theſe Re-
bukes; yet we cannot but alſo fear that there is
ſomething ſtill wanting to accompany our Supplications. And doubtleſs there are ſome particular Sins, which God is Angry with our *Iſrael*
for, that have not been duly ſeen and reſented by
us; about which God expects to be ſought if ever
he turn again our Captivity. .

Wherefore it is Commanded and Appointed,
that *Thurſday* the Fourteenth of *January* next,
be obſerved as a Day of Prayer, with Faſting
throughout this Province, ſtrictly forbidding all
Servile labour thereon; that ſo all Gods People
may offer up fervent Supplications unto him, for
the Preſervation, and Proſperity of his Majeſty's
Royal Perſon and Government, and Succeſs to
attend his Affairs both at home and abroad; that
all iniquity may be put away which hath ſtirred
God's Holy jealouſie againſt this Land; that he
would ſhew us what we know not, and help us
wherein we have done amiſs to do ſo no more;
and eſpecially that whatever miſtakes on either
hand have been fallen into, either by the body of
this People, or any orders of men, referring to
the late Tragedy, raiſed among us by Satan and

his Inſtruments, thro the awful Judgment of God, he [144] would humble us therefor and pardon all the Errors of his Servants and People, that deſire to love his Name and be attoned to his Land; that he would remove the Rod of the wicked from off the Lot of the Righteous, that he would bring the *American* Heathen, and cauſe them to hear and obey his Voice.

Given at Boſton, Decemb 17, 1696, *in the* 8*th Year of his Majeſties Reign.*

Iſaac Addington, *Secretary.*

Upon the Day of the Faſt in the full Aſſembly at the South Meeting-Houſe in *Boſton* one of the Honourable Judges,[135] who had ſat in Judicature in *Salem,* delivered in a Paper, and while it was in reading ſtood up, But the Copy being not to be obtained at preſent, It can only be reported by Memory to this effect, *viz. It was to deſire the Prayers of God's People for him and his, and that God having viſited his Family,* &c. *he was apprehenſive that he might have fallen into ſome Errors in the Matters at* Salem, *and pray that the Guilt of ſuch Miſcarriages may not be imputed either to the Country in general, or to him or his family in particular.*

---

135 The Honorable Samuel Sewall. He worſhipped at the *Old* South Church. His Name will be found inſcribed upon the Plan of the Houſe in Mr. Wiſner's *Hiſtory,* Page 102, denoting the Pew which he occupied. Its internal Arrangement is much the ſame now.

Some that had been of feveral Jewries, have given forth a Paper, Sign'd with their own hands in thefe words.

WE *whofe names are under written, being in the Year* 1692, *called to ferve as Jurors in Court at* Salem *on Tryal of many; who where by fome fufpected Guilty of doing Acts of Witchcraft upon the Bodies of fundry Perfons:*

We confefs that we ourfelves were not capable to underftand, nor able to withftand the myfterious delufions of the Powers of Darknefs, and Prince of the Air; but were for want of Knowledge in ourfelves, and better Information from others, prevailed with to take up with fuch Evidence againft the Accufed, as on further confideration, and better Information, we juftly fear was infufficient for the touching the Lives of any, Deut. xvii. 6. *whereby we fear we have been inftrumental with others, tho Ignorently and unwittingly, to bring upon ourfelves, and this People of the Lord, the Guilt of Innocent Blood; which Sin the Lord faith in Scripture, he would not pardon,* 2 Kings xxiv. 4. *that is we fuppofe in regard of his temporal Judgments. We do therefore hereby fignifie to all in general (and to the furviving Sufferers in efpecial) our deep fenfe of, and forrow for our Errors, in acting on fuch Evidence to the condemning of any perfon.*

And do hereby declare that we juftly fear that we were fadly deluded and miftaken, for which we are much difquieted and diftreffed in our minds; and do

therefore humbly beg forgivenefs, firft of God for
Chrift's fake for this our Error; And pray that
God would not impute the guilt of it to ourfelves,
nor [145] others; and we alfo pray that we may be
confidered candidly, and aright by the living Sufferers
as being then under the power of a ftrong and general
Delufion, utterly unacquainted with, and not expe-
rienced in matters of that Nature.

We do heartily afk forgivenefs of you all, whom
we have juftly offended, and do declare according to
our prefent minds, we would none of us do fuch
things again on fuch grounds for the whole World;
praying you to accept of this in way of Satisfaction
for our Offence; and that you would blefs the Inher-
itance of the Lord, that he may be entreated for the
Land.

> Foreman, *Thomas Fifk,*
> *William Fifk,*
> *John Bacheler,*
> *Thomas Fifk, Junior*
> *John Dane,*
> *Jofeph Evelith,*
> *Thomas Perly, Senior*
> *John Pebody,*
> *Thomas Perkins,*
> *Samuel Sayer,*
> *Andrew Elliott,*
> *Henry Herrick, Senior,*[136]

---

[136] Both Mather and Calef have
avoided giving Lifts of the Trial
Jurors, doubtlefs to avoid increafing
the number of their Pages. The
Records (that remain) are very im-
perfeft in this, as well as in many
other Refpeéts, already noticed. On
this Period much remains to be done.

POSTSCRIPT.

*Since making the foregoing Collettions of
Letters, to the Reverend Mr.* Cotton
Mather, *and others, &c. (which as yet
remain unanſwered) a Book is come to
hand Intituled,*

THE *Life of Sir* William Phips, *printed in*
London, 1697. Which Book, tho it bears
not the Authors name, yet the Stile, manner and
matter is ſuch, that were there no other demon-
ſtration or token to know him by, it were no
Witchcraft to determine that the ſaid Mr. *C. M.*
is the Author of it. But that he that has *en-
countred Enchantments,* and gone through the
Wonders of the Inviſible World, and *diſcovered the
Devil,* that he ſhould ſtep aſide into a Remote
Country to put on Inviſibility! Tho the reaſon
of this be not ſo manifeſt, yet it may be thought
to be to gratifie ſome peculiar fancies; and why
may not this be one, that he might with the
better grace extol the Actions of Mr. *Mather,* as
Agent in *England,* or as Preſident of *Harvard*
College, not forgetting his own.[137]

As to Sir *William,* it will be generally *acknow-*

---

[137] This Inſinuation is quite well
ſuſtained, as will appear by an Extract from Mr. Mather's Diary,
printed in Quincy's *Hiſt. H. C.*
i, 60. The Life of Phips is ſub-
ſtantially included in the Magnalia.
As originally publiſhed, it is of conſiderable rarity.

ledged that notwithſtanding the meanneſs of his
Parentage and Education, he attain'd to be Maſter of a Ship, and that he had the good hap to
find a *Spaniſh* Wreck, not only ſufficient to repair his Fortunes, but to raiſe him to a conſiderable Figure; which King *James* did ſo far ac-
commodate as to make *him a Knight.* ·

[146] And that after this, in the Reign of his
Preſent Majeſty, *he took up with thoſe of the Agents,
that were for accepting the New Charter, whereby
himſelf became Governour.*[138]

It is not doubted, but that he aimed at the
good of the People, and great Pitty it is that his
Government was ſo ſullied (for want of better
Information and Advice, from thoſe whoſe duty
it was to have given it) by that Hobgoblin Mon-
ſter, Witchcraft, whereby this Countrey was Night-
Mar'd, and harraſt, at ſuch a rate, as is not eaſily
imagined.[139]

After which ſome complaints going to *England* about Male-Adminiſtration, in the leaſt
matters comparatively; yet were ſuch, that he
was call'd home to give account thereof, where
he ſoon after expired, ſo finiſhing his Life and
Government together.[140]

[138] See Vol. I, Page 25-6.

[139] This Judgment has been ſuf-
tained by Poſterity. Phips's Hands
were tied. He could not have done
differently, had he had the Knowledge and Diſpoſition, without giving offence to Preſident Mather,
who had ſecured his Advancement.

[140] To this rather mild and in-
offenſive remark of the Author,
Mr. Mather replies: "The laſt
Effort of his [Calef's] Malice is a
Poſtſcript againſt the Life of Sir
William Phips, againſt whoſe Me-
mory, why any whoſe *Throats are
an open Sepulchre,* ſhould be ſo

Death having thus drawn the Curtain, forbidding any further Scene, it might have been prudence, to let his duſt remain without diſturbance.

But the ſaid Book -endeavouring to raiſe a Statue to him (*i. e.*) to aſcribe to him ſuch Achievements as either were never peformed by him, or elſe unduly aggravated, this has opened the Mouth, both of Friends and Enemies to recount the miſtakes in the ſaid Book; as alſo thoſe miſcarriages, wherewith Sir *William* was chargeable; ſuch as, had it not been for this Book, had been buried with him.[141]

In P. 3, ſearch is made over the World, to whom to compare him in his Advancement; and moſt unhappily *Pizarro* is pitched upon as a match for him, who was a Baſtard, dropt in a Church-Porch, put to Suck of a Sow, and being grown, ran away, and Shipt himſelf for *America*; there ſo proſpered, as to Command an Army; and therewith did mighty things, particularly took *Attaballipa*, one of the Kings of *Peru* Priſoner, and having received for his Ranſom, in Gold and Silver to the value of Ten Millions, perfidiouſly

monſtrouſly envious, that like Jackalls, they can't let him reſt quietly in his Sepulchre, good Men can't imagine any Reaſon but the third Chapter of Geneſis."—*Some Few Remarks*, &c. 47.

[141] "I have endured more than a little from ſome ſort of Men, for my writing the Life of Sir William Phips, and ſpeaking well of him, without either doing or ſpeaking ill againſt any one good Man under the whole Heavens, in the whole Compoſure. It ſeems that I muſt now write an Apology, for that Book: for which I have no Confeſſion to make, but, *That I don't wiſh one Line of it unwritten.*"—*Ibid*, 47-8.

put him to Death; and was the Death of no Man knows how many Thouſands of Innocents, and is certainly one of the worſt that could have been pitched upon for ſuch compariſon.[142]

Tho this together with the Rhetorical flouriſhes, and affected ſtrains therein, are inſtances of the Author's variety of Learning; for which he is recommended by theſe Three *Venerable* Perſon[143] in the entrance to the ſaid Book. Yet the *Integrity*, *Prudence*, and *Veracity* thereof, is not ſo manifeſtly to be ſeen. Paſſing over a multitude of Miſrepreſentations . that are therein relating to the Acts of Sir *William*, as not deſigning to rake in the Grave of the Dead, Who is it can ſee the Veracity of thoſe words? P. 40. [He lay within *Piſtol-Shot* of the Enemies Cannon, and beat them from thence, and much batter'd the town, having his Ship ſhot thro in an hundred places, with *Four and twenty Pounders*,] When in the Judgment of thoſe preſent, they were not nearer to the Enemy, than about *half or three quarters of a Mile;* that there might be in all about *Seven Shot* that [147] ſtruck the Hull of the Veſſel, none of them known to be bigger than 18 Pounders, the Enemy having but

[142] It muſt be allowed that the Doctor was a little unfortunate in his Choice of a Hero by which to meaſure his own.

[143] The "three venerable Perſons" were "Nath. Mather, John Howe and Matthew Mead." The firſt was the Uncle to Dr. Cotton Mather, then a Miniſter in Dublin, where he died a few Months later. Howe and Mead are too well known to require a notice here.

one Gun that could carry ſo big as an 18 pound Ball.[144]

It were a fondneſs after ſuch aſſertions, to take any notice of this bedeck'd Statue, when there was ſo much the leſs need of erecting one (as is aſſerted P. 108) having already been done ſo well, that even this Author himſelf deſpairs of doing it better ;[145] and that by one, a Man of ſuch diffuſed and Embalm'd a Reputation, *as that his Commendations* are aſſerted to be enough *to Immortalize* the Reputation of Sir *William,* or whomſoever elſe *he ſhould* pleaſe to beſtow them upon, *viz.* That Reverend perſon *who was* the Preſident of the only Univerſity then in the *Engliſh America,* P. 109. Which by the way is a much fairer Statue, in honour of the Preſident of the Univerſity, than that erected for Sir *William.*

For notwithſtanding all this noiſe of Erecting

---

[144] To this Dr. Mather anſwers : "When mine Adverſaries had, with a concocted Malice, done all they could, they thought at leaſt they had found one Paſſage wherein they might impeach my Veracity. I had ſaid, that before Quebeck, Sir William lay *within Piſtol Shot of the Enemies Cannon,* and that his Ship was ſhot through, in *an hundred Places,* and that it was ſhot through with *Four and Twenty Pounders.* (Tis a groſs Hardſhip for any to make my Meaning as if all the ſhot had been ſo.) And now they fall to Tragical Exclamattons ; they think *Four and Twenty Pounders* to be too ſmall Dimenſions for the Clamors they muſt batter me withal. . . . . I wrote no more than the very Words which I find in a Journal of the Expedition to Qcebec. . . . . *Calef* himſelf has lately owned, that he verily believes I did ſo."— *Some Few Remarks, &c.* 51-2.

[145] After the Doctor had ſpoken of being "battered with Clamors," he triumphantly Exclaims—"But hold *Robin,* [Mr. Calef's Chriſtian Name being Robert] I am not ſo ſoon *ſhot through ;* and the *Statue,* as I told thee, has *knock'd out thy Brains !*"—*Ibid,* Page 52. His Life of Phips he calls a *Statue.*

Statues, and the great danger in plucking them down, &c. yet in P. 89, 'tis ſaid that even Sir *William* ſhewed Choler enough, leaving it open for others, thereby to underſtand, that he was wholly given over to Paſſion and Choler.[146] And in P. 92, 'tis ſaid he did not affect any mighty ſhew of Devotion; theſe expreſſions with others may prevail with the unbiaſed Reader to think that theſe builders of Statues, had ſome further deſign in it, than to blazen the Achievements of Sir *William Phips, viz.* To ſet forth Mr. *J. Mathers* Negociation in *England,* his procuring the New-Charter for Sir *William* to be Governour, and himſelf Eſtabliſh'd Preſident of the College, are the things principally driven at in the Book.[147]

Another principal thing is to ſet forth the ſuppoſed Witchcrafts in *New-England,* and how well Mr. *Mather* the Younger therein acquitted himſelf.[148]

[146] The harſh and ungovernable Temper of the Governor was a Matter of Notoriety in his Time. See *Life of Phips in the Magnalia,* B. ii, Page 72, &c.

[147] "It is not worth our while to take Notice of every thing this *Calf* ſayes, 'tis often ſo impertinent; however, we will lay open one thing more. He ſays that Mr. Mather procured a Charter for Sir William to be Governor, and *himſelf eſtabliſhed Preſident of the Colledge.* Can there be greater Nonſenſe mixed with Malice! How could that be, when Mr. Mather had been Preſident of the Colledge *ten* Years before Sir William came to be Governor?" This is a very ſhallow Attempt to impeach, by Hypercriticiſm, the Truth of Mr. Calef's Statement. Everybody knew the fact that Dr. I. Mather was Preſident of the College. Mr. Calef's Meaning is plain enough, namely, that Mr. Mather's Solicitude was about *keeping* his Office of Preſident.

[148] "It is to be confeſſed and bewailed, that many Inhabitants of

As to the New Charter for the right under-
ſtanding that Affair, it will be needful to ſay, that
the People that afterwards ſettled in *New England,*
being about to leave their Native 'ſoil, and to ſeek
(as the Providence of God ſhould direct them)
a ſettlement in remote Regions, wherein they
might beſt ſecure their Civil and Religious Intereſts, before they enter'd upon this, conſidering
it might be needful on many accounts for their
future well being, they obtain'd a Charter to be
in the nature of a prime agreement, ſetting forth
the Soveraigns Prerogative, and the People's Priviledges; in the enjoyment whereof they long
continued, after having purchaſ'd the Title to
their Lands, of the Natives of the Country, and
ſettled themſelves therein, without any charge to
the Crown.

That Clauſe in their Charter for this Country,
viz. (Provided that no other Chriſtian Prince be
prepoſſeſt of it) being a tacit acknowledgment,
that before ſettlement no one Chriſtian Prince
had any right thereto more than another. During this time of *New-England's* Proſperity, the

New England, and young People
eſpecially, had been led away with
little *Sorceries,* wherein they *did ſe-
cretly thoſe things that were not right
againſt the Lord their God;* they
would often cure Hurts with *Spells,*
and practice deteſtable Conjurations
with *Sieves,* and *Keyes,* and *Peaſe,*
and *Nails,* and *Horſe-ſhoes,* and other
Implements to learn the Things for
which they had a forbidden and im-
pious Curioſity. Wretched Books
had ſtolen into the Land, wherein
Fools were inſtructed how to become able Fortune-tellers."—*Life
of Sir W. Phips.* See *Magnalia,*
B. ii, 60. Some twenty Years later
the Author's Ideas had undergone a
ſlight Change. See *Remarkables,*
161, *et ſeq.*

Government here were very ſparing of Granting Freedoms, except to ſuch as [148] were ſo and ſo qualſied. Whereby the number of *Non*-Freemen[149] being much increaſ'd, they were very uneaſie, by their being ſhut out from having any ſhare in the Government, or having any Votes for their Repreſentatives, *&c.* it rendred many of them ready to join with ſuch as were undermining the Government, not duly conſidering that it had been far more ſafe to have endeavoured to prevail with the Legiſlators for an enlargement.

So that it will not be wonder'd at that in the latter end of the Reign of King *Charles* the II. and of King *James*, (when moſt of the Charters in *England* were vacated) that this was *quo warranto'd* and finally Judgment entered up againſt it, and the Country was put into ſuch a form of Government as was moſt agreeable to thoſe times, *viz.* A Legiſlative pow'r was lodg'd in the Governour (or Preſident) and ſome few appointed to be of his Counſel, without any regard therein, either to the Laws of *England*, or thoſe formerly of this Colony : Thus rendering the Circumſtances of this Country beyond compariſon worſe than thoſe of any Corporation in *England*. The People of thoſe Corporations being acknowledged ſtill to have a right to *Magna Charta*, when their particular Charters were made void. But here

---

149 Complete Liſts of all the Free-men in Maſſachuſetts, and the Qualifications neceſſary to become ſuch, will be found in the *New Eng. Hiſt. aud Gen. Regiſter*, Vols. III, IV and VII.

when *Magna Charta* has been pleaded, the People have been anſwered, that they muſt not expeᶜt that *Magna Charta* would follow them to the end of the World: not only their Eſtates, but their Lives being thereby rendered wholly precarious. And Judge *Palmer*[150] has ſet forth in Print, that the King has power to grant ſuch a Commiſſion over this People.

It is not hard to imagine that under ſuch a Commiſſion, not only the People were liable to be oppreſt by Taxes, but alſo by Confiſcations, and Siezing of Lands, unleſs Patents were purchaſed at Exceſſive prizes, with many other Exorbitant Innovations.

The firſt that accepted this Commiſſion was Mr. *Dudley,* a Gentleman born in this Country, who did but prepare the way for Sir *Edm. Andros.* In whoſe time things being grown to ſuch Extremities, not only here, but in *England,* as render'd the ſucceeding Revolution abſolutely neceſſary; the Revolution here being no other than an aᶜting according to the Precedent given by *England.*

During the time of Sir *Edmonds'* Government,

---

[150] Palmer's Book is thus entitled: "An Impartial Account of the State of New England: or, the Late Government there, Vindicated. In Anſwer to the Declaration which the Faᶜtion ſet forth, when they Overturned that Government. With a Relation of the Horrible Uſage they treated the Governour with, and his Council; and all that had His Majeſty's Commiſſion. *In a* Letter *to the* Clergy *there.* By *John Palmer.* London: Printed for *Edward Poole,* at the *Ship* over againſt the *Royal Exchange,* in *Cornhill,* 1690." 4to, 40 Pages. This Work is about to be republiſhed by the PRINCE SOCIETY.

Mr. *Increaſe Mather*, Teacher of the North
Church in *Boſton*, having undergone ſome trouble
by Fobb-Actions[151] laid upon him, &c. (tho with
ſome difficulty) he made his Eſcape, and got paſſage for *England*, being therein aſſiſted by ſome
particular Friends; where being arrived, he applied himſelf to King *James* for redreſs of thoſe
Evils the Country then groaned under; and
meeting with a ſeeming kind reception, and ſome
promiſes, it was as much as might at that time be
reaſonably expected.[152]

[149] Upon the Day of the Revolution here,
tho the greateſt part of the People were for reaſſuming their Ancient Government, purſuant to
his Royal Highneſs' Proclamation; yet matters
were ſo clog'd, that the People were diſſmiſt
without it, who did not in the leaſt miſtruſt but
that thoſe who were put out of the Government
by Mr. *Dudley*, would reaſſume: Mr. *Broadſtreet*,
who had been then Governour, being heard to
ſay that Evening, when returned home, *That had
not he thought they would have reaſſum'd, he would*

---

151 Actions brought without Foundation.

152 " The Superior Gentlemen in
the Oppreſſed Country, thought,
that a Well-qualified Perſon going
over with the Addreſſes of the
Churches to the King, might, by
the Help of ſuch Proteſtant Diſ-
ſenters as the King began upon
Political Views to caſt a fair Aſpect
upon, obtain ſome Relief to the
growing Diſtreſſes of the Country;
and Mr. Mather was the Perſon
that was pitch'd upon. . . . . . To
his Wonderment, they that at another Time would have almoſt af-
ſoon parted with their Eyes as have
parted with him now were willing
to it."—*Remarkables of Dr. I. Mather*, 103.

not have ſtirr'd out of his Houſe that Day.[153]   But
after this, ſome that were driving at other matters,
had opportunities by Threats and other ways not
only to prevail with that good Old Gentleman,
but with the reſt of the Government wholly to
decline it; which ſome few obſerving, they took
the opportunity to call themſelves a Committee
of Safety, and ſo undertook to Govern ſuch as
would be govern'd by them.[154]

It has been an Obſervation of long continuance
*that matters of State ſeldom proſper, when managed
by the Clergy.*   Among the oppoſers of the reaſſuming few were ſo ſtrenuous as ſome of the
Miniſters, and among the Miniſters none more
vehement than Mr. *Cotton Mather,* Paſtor of the
North Church in *Boſton,* who has charged them
as they would anſwer it another day to reaſſume.
Among his Arguments againſt it, one was that it
would be to put a ſlight upon his Father, who,
he ſaid, was in *England,* labouring for a compleat
Reſtoration of Charter Privileges, not doubting,
but they would be ſpeedily obtain'd.   Any Man
that knows *New England* cannot but be ſenſible,
that ſuch Diſcourſes from ſuch Men, have always
been very prevalent.   And hence it was that even

---

[153] Mr. Bradſtreet was then about
86 Years of Age.   A pretty full
Account of the Tranſactions of this
Period may be read in Hutchinſon, *Hiſt. Maſs.,* i, *ſub. An.* 1689:
" The Repreſentatives of 54 Towns
met at Boſton, on the 22d of May.

They ſoon diſcovered a Deſire to
reaſſume the Charter.   The major
Part of the Council were againſt
it."   *Ibid.,* i, 386, firſt Edition.

[154] I do not find this animad-
verted upon in the *Some Few Remarks.*

thoſe that would think themſelves wronged, if they were not numbred among the beſt Friends to *New-England,* and to its Charter, would not ſo much as ſtoop to take it up, when there was really nothing to hinder them from the Enjoyment thereof.[155]

After the Committee of Safety had continued about ſeven Weeks, or rather after Anarchy had been ſo long Triumphant, an Aſſembly having been call'd came to this reſolve and laid it before thoſe Gentlemen that had been of the Government, that if they would not act upon the Foundation of the Charter, that perſuant to it, the Aſſembly would appoint ſome others in that Station. The Anſwer to which was, that they would accept, *&c.* And when a Declaration ſignifying ſuch a reaſſuming, was prepared with the good liking of the Deputies, in order to be publiſhed, ſome that were oppoſers, ſo terrified thoſe Gentlemen, that before publiſhing it was underwritten [that they would not have it underſtood that they did reaſſume Charter-Government] to the no ſmall amazement of the People, and diſappointment of the Deputies, who if theſe had not promiſed ſo to act, had taken other care, and put in thoſe that would.[156]

[155] See Neal's *Hiſt. N. England,* where will be found the "Declaration" in full, in which it is ſaid: "Having fully and deliberately examined the Minds and Inſtructions of the ſeveral Towns, do find it to be the general Conſent and Con-currence of our ſeveral Towns to reaſſume the Government according to Charter-Rights," &c. Vol. II, 55.

[156] The *underwritten* Recantation does not appertain to the printed Declaration. Neal ſays: "'Tis certain the Maſſachuſet-

[150] The next principal thing done was, they choſe two of their Members, *viz.* one of the upper Houſe, the other of the lower, both of them Gentlemen of known Integrity, as well as ability to go to *England,* in order to obtain their Reſettlement ;[157] and in regard Mr. *I. Mather* was already there, they joined him, as alſo a certain Gentleman in *London*[158] with theſe other two : Thoſe from hence being arrived in *London,* they all united for the common Intereſt of the Countrey, though without the deſired effect. They were in doubt, whether it were beſt to Improve their Utmoſt for a reverſal of the Judgment in a Courſe of Law, or to obtain it in a Parliamentary way, or to Petition his Majeſty for a New Grant of former Priviledges ; And conſidering that the two firſt might prove Dilatory and Expenſive, as well as for other reaſons, they reſolved upon the latter, and Petition'd his Majeſty for the Countries Reſettlement, with former Privileges, and what further additionals his Majeſty in his Princely Wiſdom ſhould think fit. Accordingly it pleaſed his Majeſty to declare in Counſel his Determination, *viz.* That there ſhould be a Charter granted to *New-England.* But the Minutes then taken thereof, and a Draught of the *New-Charter* being ſeen, it was the Opinion of the two Gentlemen

---

Provinces had hard Meaſure in the Loſs of their Charter, and harder yet, in not having it reſtored at the Revolution," &c. Vol. II, 59.

[157] Eliſha Cooke and Thomas Oakes, both of them Aſſiſtants. See Hutchinſon, *Hiſt. Maſs.,* i, 393.
[158] Sir Henry Aſhurſt.

ſent from hence, that it were beſt to tarry his Majeſties return from *Flanders ;* in hopes then to obtain eaſe in ſuch things as might be any ways deemed to be grievous. And this was the reſult of the Advice of ſuch as were beſt able to give it, that they could meet with, and accordingly they wholly deſiſted taking it out of the Offices.[159]

But Mr. *Mather* and that other Gentleman had, as it is ſaid, other advice given them, which they ſtrenuouſly purſued, and his Majeſty having left it as is aſſerted in this of the Life of Sir *William*, P. 57, to them to nominate a Governour, they pitcht upon Sir *William Phips*, who was then in *England*, [As the moſt likely and able to ſerve the King's Intereſts among the People there ; under the changes in ſome things unacceptable now brought upon them, P. 62.] and

[159] Dr. J Mather's Narrative of this Affair runs thus: "When the King was pleaſed to give a poſitive Command that the Charter of New England ſhould be diſpatched, it was not for the Agents to ſay, It ſhall not be ſo. True it is, that all the Agents, when they ſaw what Minutes would be inſerted in the Charter, were deſirous of a Delay, until the Kings happy Return to England. And I may without Vanity ſay, no Man laboured to have it ſo, more than myſelf. I prayed Arch-Biſhop Tillotſon to intercede with the Queen for this Favour to us, who at my Requeſt did ſo. Moreover, I drew up ſeveral Reaſons againſt that which in the Minutes of the New Charter is moſt grievous to us; which were by Sir Henry Aſhurſt, and my ſelf, delivered to His Majeſties Attourney General, on July 24. 1691, and which I did alſo ſend to my Lord Sidney, one of His Majeſties principal Secretaries of State, then with the King in Flanders."—*Some Few Remarks*, 22-3. Lord Henry *Sydney* was afterwards Earl of Romney.

without tarrying for the concurrence of thoſe other Agents, the Charter was taken out, &c.[160]

But Mr. *Mather* perhaps fearing he ſhould have but ſmall thanks here, for his having ſo far an hand in bringing upon them thoſe unacceptable Changes, wrote, and cauſed to be Printed, an Account of his Negotiation, but ſurely by ſome Error in the Conception, it proved only an *Embrio*, and was ſtifled as ſoon as born. One indeed, deſigned to be as it were a *Poſthumous* was left with Mr. *Bailey*, formerly of *Boſton*, and a Member of the *North-Church*, with a charge not to ſuffer it to be ſeen till he were gone to *New-England;* yet it ſeems ſome other perſon got a ſight of it, which was the occaſion of Mr. *Mather*'s ſending him that Minatory Epiſtle, by ſome call'd a Bull. But beſides this, for fear of the worſt, Mr. *Mather* got ſeveral *Non-con* Miniſters to give him a Teſtimonial, or Letters of Commendations for his great Service herein.[161]

[151] In the mean time Mr. *Cotton Mather*, being in ſome doubt of the ſame thing, handed

---

[160] Thinking there would be no further Proceedings about the Charter before the Return of the King, Mr. Mather ſays he went into the Country for the Recovery of his impaired Health, where, before he had been three Weeks, he was ſurpriſed by being ſent for to London, " with Information that the King had ſignified His Royal Pleaſure to the Earl of Nottingham, that there ſhould be a Procedure with a Char-ter for the Maſſachuſetts Colony, according to the Minutes that the Lords of the Committee for Plantations had agreed to, notwithſtanding the Objections of the Agents."— *Some Few Remarks*, 23.

[161] This Document is printed in the Work juſt cited, Pages 14 to 18; and alſo by the Son in his *Remarkables* of his Father, Pages 157-60. The rebutting of the " Bull" has been noticed in an earlier Page.

about a Paper of Fables; wherein his Father under the Name of *Mercurius,* and himſelf under the Name of *Orpheus,* are extoll'd, and the great Actions of *Mercurius* magnified; the preſent Charter exalted, by trampling on the former, as being very defective, and all thoſe call'd unreaſonable that did not readily agree with the New one: And indeed the whole Country are compared to no better than Beaſts, except *Mercurius* and *Orpheus,* the Governour himſelf muſt not Eſcape being termed an Elephant, tho as good as he was great, and the Inferiours told by *Orpheus* that for the quiet Enjoyment of their Lands, &c. they were beholding to *Mercurius.* Tho this Paper was judged not convenient to be Printed, yet ſome Copies were taken, the Author having ſhown variety of *Heathen* Learning in it.[162]

This is in ſhort that eminent Service for which the ſaid Mr. *I. M.* is in the preſent Book ſo highly extol'd. In ſo many Pages, that to repeat them were to tranſcribe a conſiderable part of the ſaid Book.

And no doubt he deſerves as much thanks as Dr. *Sharp*[163] did, when he was ſent by the Preſ-

---

[162] Whether this Paper, containing the *variety of Heathen Learning,* was ever printed, the Editor is unable to ſay.

[163] The Defenders of Dr. Mather ſay, that, by what they have heard about that Story of Dr. Sharp, attempting "to get himſelf made Biſhop, did what he could to undermine the Preſbyterian Government:" and continue,—"Certainly, Satan *himſelf* could not but bluſh to ſay, that ever Mr. Mather went to deſtroy the Government of New England, either as to their Civil or Eccleſiaſtical Conſtitution." —*Some Few Remarks,* 29, 30. Mr. Calef is very far from bringing any

bytery of *Scotland,* to procure the ſettlement of their Kirk by King *Charles* II. at his Reſtauration.

Not but that the preſent Charter of *New-England* is indeed truly valuable, as containing in it peculiar Priviledges, which abundantly Engages this People to pay the tribute of thankfulneſs to his Majeſty,[164] and all due ſubjection to whom it ſhall pleaſe him to ſubſtitute as Governour over us; and to pray that the King of Kings would pour out of his richeſt bleſſings upon him, giving him a long and proſperous Reign over the Nations, under the benign Influences whereof, Oppreſſion and Tyranny may flee away.

And if his Majeſty hath put this People into the preſent form of Government, to the end they might be in the better condition of Defence in a time of War; or that they might the better underſtand the Priviledge of chooſing their own Governour by the want of it, and ſhould be graciouſly pleaſed (the War being over) to reſtore to theſe, as has been already granted to the reſt of his Majeſties Subjects, the full employment of their Ancient Priviledges, it would be ſuch an obligation upon them to thankfulneſs and Duty

·ſuch Charge. Some later Authors are far more ſevere on Dr. Mather than he. See Baylies, *N. Plymouth,* iv, 134.

164 After extracting this Acknowledgement of our Author, his Reviewers ſay: "With what Face then can he inſinuate that no Thanks are due to the Inſtruments of obtaining ſuch a valuable Charter, and ſo many peculiar Priviledges? Surely he was beſide himſelf, when he wrote ſuch Things as theſe.—*Ibid.,* Page 30.

as could never be forgotten, nor fufficiently expreft, and would rather abate than increafe charge
to the Crown.

As to the fuppofed Witchcrafts in *New-England*, having already faid fo much thereof, there
is the lefs remains to be added.

In the times of Sir *Ed. Andros* his Government,
Goody *Glover*, a defpifed, crazy, ill-conditioned
old Woman, an *Irifh Roman* Catholick, was tried
for Afflicting *Goodwins* Children ; by the Account
of which Tryal, taken in Short-hand, for the ufe
of the Jury, it may appear that the ge[152]neral-
ity of her Anfwers, were Nonfenfe, and her behaviour like that of one diftracted. Yet the Drs. finding her as fhe had been for many Years, brought
her in *Compos Mentis ;* and fetting afide her crazy
Anfwers to fome infnaring queftions, the proof
againft her was wholly deficient : The Jury
brought her Guilty.[165]

[165] The Authors of the *Some Few Remarks*, print a Letter from Mr. John Goodwin, as a triumphant Vindication of what Dr. Cotton Mather publifhed refpecting the bewitchment of Goodwin's Children. The Letter is too long and too unimportant to occupy Space here. It may be feen on Pages 62 and 63 of that Work. It is, of courfe, an attempt to fuftain Dr. Mather's Account, the fubftance of which Account is in the *Magnalia*. They then go on : "Now behold how active and forward Mr. Mather was, in tranfacting the Affairs relating to this Woman ; and be aftonifhed, that ever any *One* fhould go to infinuate things to the World, as are known by moft that ever heard of thofe afflicted Children, to be fo far different from *Truth*, as to do what in you lies to leffen the Efteem of thofe Servants of Chrift, (which you make your chiefeft *Butts*) among the Lord's People. . . . . We pray God *Pardon* your Sin, and give you the Grace to Repent."—*Ibid*, 65. See alfo *Magnalia*, B. ii, 61, where it appears that Mr. Jofeph Dudley was Chief Judge when the poor old crazy Woman was tried and Executed.

Mr. *Cotton Mather* was the moft active and
forward of any Minifter in the Country in thofe
matters, taking home one of the Children, and
managing fuch intreagues with that Child, and
after printing fuch an Account of the whole, in
his Memorable Providences, as conduced much
to the kindling thofe Flames, that in Sir *Williams* time threatned the devouring this Country.[166]

King *Saul* in his deftroying the Witches out of
Ifrael, is thought by many to have exceeded, and
in his Zeal to have flain the *Gibeonites* wrongfully
under that notion : Yet went after this to a Witch
to know his Fortune. For his wrongful deftroying the *Gibeonites* (befides the Judgments of
God upon the Land) his Sons were hanged ; and
for his going to the Witch, himfelf was cut off.
Our fir *William Phips* did not do this, but as appears by this Book had firft his Fortune told him,
(by fuch as the Author counts no better) and

[166] Dr. Mather anfwers : "After the Storm was raifed at Salem,
I did myfelf offer to provide Meat,
Drink, and Lodging, for no lefs
than *Six* of the Afflicted, that fo an
Experiment might be made, whether
Prayer with *Fafting,* upon the Removal of thofe Miferables, one from
another, might not put a Period unto
the Trouble then arifing, without giving the Civil Authority the Trouble
of Profecuting the Methods of the
Law on that Occafion. You'll fay,
How came it then to pafs that many
People took up another Notion of
me ? Truly, *Satan knows.* Perhaps 'twas becaufe I thought it my
Duty alwayes to fpeak of the Honourable Judges with as much Honour as I could ; (a Crime which I
am generally taxed for, and *for which
I hav ebeen finely requited !*) This
made People, who judge of Things
at a Diftance, to dream that I *approved* of all that was done."—
Ibid, 39-40. Certainly, if Words
mean any thing, what he publifhed
fully juftifies that Conclufion, notwithftanding his rare *Ambidexterity.*
See Vol. I, *Ubique loci.*

though he put it off (to his Paſtor, who he new
approved not thereof) as if it were brought to
him in writing, without his ſeeking, &c. Yet
by his bringing it ſo far, and ſafe keeping it ſo
many Years, it appears he made ſome Account of
it; for which he gave the Writer, after he had
found the Wreck, as a reward, more than Two
hundred pounds. His telling his Wife (P. 6.)
that he ſhould be a Commander, ſhould have a
Brick-Houſe in *Greenlane*,[167] &c. might be in
confidence of ſome ſuch Prediction, and that he
could foretel to him (P. 90.) that he ſhould
be Governour of *New-England*, was probably
ſuch an one, (the Scriptures not having re-
vealed it.) Such Predictions would have been
counted at *Salem*, pregnant proofs of Witchcraft,
and much better than what were againſt ſeveral
that ſuffered there. But Sir *William*, when the
Witchcrafts at *Salem* began (in his Eſteem) to
look formidable, that he might Act ſafely in this
Affair, he aſked the Advice of the Miniſters in
and near *Boſton;* the whole of their Advice and
Anſwer is Printed in *Caſes of Conſcience*, the laſt
Pages. But left the World ſhould be Ignorant
who it was that drew the ſaid Advice, in this
Book of the Life of Sir *William Phips*, P. 77. are
theſe words, *the Miniſters made unto his Excellency
and the Counſel a return, drawn up at their deſire,*

---

[167] Salem Street was in thoſe
Times, called *Green-Lane;* at the
Corner made by that *Lane* and
Charter Streeet, the Governor ac-
tually reſided. See *Hiſtory and
Antiquities of Reaſon*, 816.

by Mr. Mather *the Younger, as I have been informed.* Mr. *C. M.* therein intending to beguile
.the World, and make them think that another,
and not himſelf had taken that notice of his
(ſuppoſed) good Service done therein, which
otherwiſe would have been aſcribed to thoſe
Miniſters in General, though indeed the Advice
then given, looks moſt like a thing of his Com-
poſing, as carrying both Fire [153] to increaſe,
and Water to quench the Conflagration.[168] Particularly after the Devils Teſtimony, by the ſuppoſed Afflicted had ſo prevailed, as to take away
the Life of one, and the Liberty of an Hundred,
and the whole Country ſet into a moſt dreadful
conſternation, then this Advice is given, uſhered
in with thanks for what was already done, and
in concluſion, putting the Government upon a
ſpeedy and vigorous proſecution according to the
Laws of God, and the wholeſome Statutes of the
Engliſh Nation, ſo adding Oil, rather than Water
to the Flame; for who ſo little acquainted with
proceedings of *England,* as not to know that they
have taken ſome methods, with thoſe here uſed
to diſcover who were Witches. The reſt of the

---

[168] Dr. Mather ſays in Reply:
"Moreover, when the Miniſters
preſented unto the Governour and
Council, their Advice againſt making the *Spectral Exhibitions* to be
ſo much as a *Preſumption of Witchcraft,* it was *my* poor Hand which
drew up that Advice, and my Heart
was always in it."—*Some Few Re-*
marks, 38-9. But the Doctor does
not explain how, in ſpeaking of this
Addreſs in the Life of Phips, he
came to make uſe of the Words—
as I have been informed—while in
the *Some Few Remarks* he owns
that. it was drawn by his *poor Hand.*
See *Life of Phips in Magnalia,*
Book II, 63.

Advice, conſiſting of cautions and directions, are
inſerted in this of the Life of Sir *William.* So
that if Sir *William,* looking upon the thanks for
what was paſt, and Exhortation to proceed, went
on to take away the Lives of Nineteen more,
this is according to the Advice ſaid to be given
him by the Miniſters, and if the Devil after
thoſe Executions be affronted, by diſbelieving his
teſtimony, and by clearing and Pardoning all the
reſt of the Accuſed ; yet this alſo is according to
that Advice, but to caſt the Scale ; the ſame that
drew this Advice, ſaith, in *Wonders of the Inviſible World, Enchantments Encountered;* [that to
have a hand in any thing that may ſtifle or ob-
ſtruct a regular detection of that Witchcraft, is
what we may well with a Holy fear avoid :
Their Majeſties good Subjects muſt not every
day be torn to pieces by horrid Witchcraft, and
thoſe bloody Felons be wholly left unproſecuted;
The Witchcraft is a buſineſs that will not be
ſhamm'd.][169] The Paſtor of that Church, of
which Sir *William* was a Member, being of
this Principle, and thus declaring it, after the
former advice; no wonder tho it caſt the Scale
againſt thoſe Cautions. It is rather a Wonder
that no more Blood was ſhed, for if that Advice
of his Paſtors could ſtill have prevail'd with the
Governour, Witchcraft had not been ſo ſhammed
off as it was. Yet now in this Book of the Life
of Sir *William,* the pardoning the Priſoners when

169 See Volume I, Page 34.

Condemn'd, and clearing the Goals, is call'd (P.
82) a Vanquiſhing the Devil, adding this Con-
queſt to the reſt of the Noble Atchievements of
Sir *William*, tho Performed not only without,
but directly againſt his Paſtors Advice. But this
is not all, tho this Book pretends to raiſe a Statue
in Honour of Sir *William*, yet it appears it was the
leaſt part of the deſign of the Author to Honour
him, but it was rather to Honour himſelf, and the
Miniſters; It being ſo unjuſt to Sir *William*, as
to give a full Account of the cautions given him,
but deſignedly hiding from the Reader the In-
couragements and Exhortations to proceed, that
were laid before him (under the name of the
Miniſters Advice) in effect, telling the World
that thoſe Executions at *Salem*, were without,
and againſt the Advice of the Miniſters, expreſt
in thoſe Cautions, purpoſely hiding their giving
thanks for what was already done, and exhorting
to proceed; thereby rendering Sir *William* of ſo
ſanguin a Complexion, that the Miniſters had
ſuch cauſe to fear his going on with the Tragedy,
tho againſt their Advice; that they deſired the
Preſident to write his *Caſes of Conſcience, &c.*
To plead miſinformation will not ſalve here,
however it may ſeem to palliate other things, but
is a manifeſt, deſigned traverſty, or miſrepreſent-
ation of the Miniſters Advice to Sir *William*, a
hiding the truth, and a wronging the dead, whom
the Author ſo much pretends to honour; for
which the Acknowledgments ought to be as
Univerſal as the offence. But tho the Miniſters

Advice, or rather Mr. *C. Mather's* was perfectly
Ambidexter, giving as great or greater Encouragement to proceed in thofe dark methods, than
cautions againft [154] them; yet many Eminent
perfons being accufed, there was a neceffity of a
ftop to be put to it. If it be true what was faid
at the Counfel-board in anfwer to the commendations of Sir *William*, for his ftopping the proceedings about Witchcraft, *viz.* That it was high
time for him to ftop it, his own Lady being accufed; if that Affertion were a truth, then *New-
England* may feem to be more beholden to the
accufers for accufing of her, and thereby neceffi-
tating a ftop, than to Sir *William*, or to the Advice
that was given him by his Paftor.[170]

Mr. *C. M.* having been very forward to write
Books of Witchcraft, has not been fo forward
either to explain or defend the Doctrinal part
thereof, and his belief (which he had a Years
time to compofe) he durft not venture fo as to be
copied.[171] Yet in this of the Life of Sir *William*
he fufficiently teftifies his retaining that Hetero-
dox belief, feeking by frightfull ftories of the
fufferings of fome, and the refined fight of others,
&c. P. 69 to obtrude upon the World, and con-

---

[170] Dr. Douglafs goes further in
this Matter. He fays that "fome
of the Confeffing Witches, by over-
acting their Parts in accufing fome
of Gov. Phips's, and the Rev. Mr.
Mather's Relations; as alfo fome of
the Accufed good Chriftians, and
of good Eftates, thofe arrefted the
Accufers in high Actions for Defa-
mation; this put a ftop to Accufations."—*Summary*, i, 450.

[171] Referring to certain Anfwers
in writing put into Mr. Calef's
Hands, with an Injunction againft
his printing them. See *ante*, Vol. II,
Page 86.

firm it in ſuch a belief, as hitherto he either cannot or will not defend, as if the Blood already ſhed thereby were not ſufficient.[172]

Mr. *I. Mather*, in his *Caſes of Conſcience*, P. 25, tells of a Bewitched Eye, and that ſuch can ſee more than others. They were certainly bewitched Eyes that could ſee as well ſhut as open, and that could ſee what never was, that could ſee the Priſoners upon the Afflicted, harming of them, when thoſe whoſe Eyes were not bewitched could have ſworn that they did not ſtir from the Bar. The Accuſers are ſaid to have ſuffered much by biting, P. 73. And the prints of juſt ſuch a ſet of Teeth, as thoſe they Accuſed, had, but ſuch as had not ſuch bewitch'd Eyes have ſeen the Accuſers bite themſelves, and then complain of the Accuſed. It has alſo been ſeen when the Accuſed, inſtead of having juſt ſuch a ſet of Teeth, has not had

---

[172] This Statement is fully borne out, as will be ſeen on referring to the Life of Phips, as directed above, or to the ſame in the *Magnalia*, B. ii, 60, *et ſeq. ;* one Extract here muſt ſuffice : " But of all the *Preternatural* things which befel theſe People, there were none more unaccountable than thoſe, wherein the preſtigious *Dæmons* would ever now and then cover the moſt *Corporeal* Things in the World with a *Faſcinating Miſt* of Inviſibility. As now; a Perſon was cruelly aſſaulted by a *Spectre*, that, ſhe ſaid, run at her with a *Spindle*, though no Body elſe in the Room could ſee either the *Spectre* or the *Spindle :* At laſt, in her Agonies, giving a Snatch at the *Spectre*, ſhe pulled the *Spindle* away ; and it was no ſooner got into her Hand, but the other Folks then preſent beheld that it was indeed a Real, Proper, Iron *Spindle ;* which, when they locked up very ſafe, it was nevertheleſs by the *Dæmons* taken away to do farther Miſchief." In the *Wonders of the Inviſible World* (Vol. I, 205), this Story of the Spindle will be ſeen among the *Curioſities*, and is given, as the Author there tells the Reader, as "a Bone to pick" for the *Dogmatical. See alſo* Lawſon, 102.

one in his head.[173] They were ſuch bewitched Eyes that could ſee the Poiſonous Powder (brought by Spectres P. 70.) And that could ſee in the Aſhes the print of the Brand, there inviſibly heate to torment the pretended Sufferers with, &c.[174]

Theſe with the reſt of ſuch Legends have this direct tendency, *viz.* To tell the World that the Devil is more ready to ſerve his Votaries, by his doing for them things above or againſt the courſe of Nature, ſhewing himſelf to them, and making explicit contract with them, &c. than the Divine Being is to his faithful Servants, and that as he is

---

[173] It is highly intereſting to hear the Doctor's Account of this: "It was alſo found, that the Fleſh of the Afflicted was often *Bitten* at ſuch a Rate, that not only the *Print of Teeth* would be left on their *Fleſh*, but the very *Slaver* of *Spittle* too: As there would appear juſt ſuch a *ſet of Teeth* as was in the *Accuſed*, even ſuch as might be clearly diſtinguiſhed from other People's. And uſually the *Afflicted* went through a terrible Deal of ſeeming Difficulties from the tormenting *Spectres*, and muſt be long waited on before they could get a Breathing Space from their Tormentors to give in their Teſtimonies."—*Life of Phips, in Magnalia,* B. ii, 61-2.

[174] The Doctor muſt once again be heard, otherwiſe the Reader can have but a faint Idea of what our Author is expoſing: "The Miſera-

ble exclaimed extreamly of *Branding Irons* heating at the Fire on the Hearth to mark them; now, though the Standers by could ſee no *Irons*, yet they could ſee diſtinctly the Print of them in the Aſhes, and *ſmell* them too as they were carried by the *not-ſeen Furies*, unto the poor Creatures for whom they were intended; and thoſe poor Creatures were thereupon *Stigmatized* with them, that they will bear the Marks of them to their Dying Day. Nor are theſe the *Tenth Part* of the *Prodigies* that fell out among the Inhabitants of New England."—*Ibid.*, Page 61. If any one, after reading theſe ſtrongly expreſſed Opinions of the learned Doctor, will entertain Doubts, as to his extreme Credulity and Faith in Witchcraft, it is not likely to be in human Power to remove them.

W8

willing, ſo alſo able to perform their deſires.[175] The way whereby theſe People are believed to arrive at a power to Afflict their Neighbours, is by a compact with the Devil, and that they have a power to *Commiſſionate* him to thoſe Evils, P. 72. However Irrational, or inſcriptural ſuch Aſſertions are, yet they ſeem a neceſſary part of the *Faith* of ſuch as maintain the belief of ſuch a ſort of *Witches*.

As the Scriptures know nothing of a covenanting or commiſſioning Witch, ſo Reaſon cannot conceive how Mortals ſhould by their Wickedneſs arrive at a power to Commiſſionate Angels, Fallen Angels, againſt their Innocent Neighbours. But the Scriptures are full in it, and the Inſtances numerous, that the Almighty, Divine Being has this prerogative to make uſe of what Inſtrument he pleaſeth, in Afflicting any, and conſequently to commiſſionate Devils : And tho this word commiſſioning, in the Authors former Books, might be thought to be by inadvertency, yet now after he hath been caution'd of it, ſtill to perſiſt in it ſeems highly Criminal. And therefore in the name of God, I here charge ſuch belief as guilty of Sacrilege in the higheſt Nature, and ſo much worſe than ſtealing Church Plate, *&c.* As it is

---

[175] The Cry of " Blaſphemer, Sadducee, Infidel, Liar, Slanderer," &c., &c., could not then, nor at any other Time, alter the Facts ſo truly and ſo ſuccinctly ſtated here. Againſt the above is found : " He infinuates, that our Reverend Miniſters make the Devil an *Independent Being*, and (as he ſays) *conſequently a God*. An abominable Charge !" —*Some Few Remarks*, 8, 9. See, alſo, Vol. I, Page 72-3.

a higher Offence to ſteal any of the glorious Attributes of the Al[155]mighty, to beſtow them upon Mortals, than it is to ſteal the Utenſils appropriated to his Service. And whether to aſcribe ſuch power of commiſſioning Devils to the worſt of Men, be not direct Blaſphemy, I leave to others better able to determine. When the Phariſees were ſo wicked as to aſcribe to *Beelzebub*, the mighty works of Chriſt (whereby he did manifeſtly ſhew forth his Power and Godhead) than it was that our Saviour declar'd the Sin againſt the Holy Ghoſt to be unpardonable.

When the Righteous God is contending with Apoſtate Sinners, for their departures from him, by his Judgments, as Plagues, Earthquakes, Storms and Tempeſts, Sickneſſes and Diſeaſes, Wars, loſs of Cattle, *&c.* Then not only to aſcribe this to the Devil, but to charge one another with ſending or commiſſionating thoſe Devils to theſe things, is ſo abominable and ſo wicked, that it requires a better Judgment than mine to give it its juſt denomination.[176]

But that Chriſtians ſo called ſhould not only charge their fellow Chriſtians therewith, but pro-

---

[176] And yet, as inconſiſtent with Reaſon as this abſurd Stuff is, it was the generally prevailing Belief, and is thus *defended* in the *Some Few Remarks*, P. 8 : "The whole Body of the Miniſters in the Country are charged, as Guilty of Sacriledge in the higheſt Degree, if not direct Blaſphemy, and Diabolical Wickedneſs." It will at once be ſeen that this is as unjuſt a Charge as Malignity in its Blindneſs could invent. Well did our Quaker Poet write, ſome 17 Years ago :

"When the Thought of Man is free,
  Error fears its lighteſt Tones;
So the Prieſt cried 'Sadducee!'
  And the People took up Stones."

ceed to Trials and Executions; crediting that Enemy to all Goodneſs, and Accuſer of the Brethren, rather than believe their Neighbours in their own Defence; this is ſo Diabolical a Wickedneſs as cannot proceed, but from a Doctrine of Devils; how far damnable it is let others diſcuſs. Though ſuch things were acting in this Country in Sir *Williams* time, yet P. 65. There is a Diſcourſe of a Guardian Angel, as then over-ſeeing it, which notion, however it may ſuit the Faith of *Ethnicks,* or the fancies of *Trithemius;* it is certain that the Omnipreſent Being, ſtands not in need as Earthly Potentates do, of governing the World by Vicegerents. And if Sir *William* had ſuch an Inviſible pattern to imitate, no wonder though ſome of his Actions were unaccountable, eſpecially thoſe relating to Witchcraft : For if there was in thoſe Actions an Angel ſuperintending, there is little reaſon to think it was *Gabriel* or the Spirit of *Mercury,* nor *Hanael* the Angel or Spirit of *Venus,* nor yet *Samuel* the Angel or Spirit of *Mars;* Names feigned by the ſaid *Trithemius, &c.* It may rather be thought to be *Apollyon,* or *Abaddon.*

Obj. But here it will be ſaid, What are there no Witches? Do's not the Law of God command that they ſhould be extirpated? Is the Command vain and Unintelligible? *Sol.* For any to ſay that a Witch is one that makes a compact with, and Commiſſions Devils, *&c.* is indeed to render the Law of God vain and Unintelligible, as having provided no way whereby they might be detected, and proved to be fuch; And how the *Jews* waded thro this difficulty for fo 'many Ages, without the Supplement of Mr. *Perkins* and *Bernard* thereto, would be very myfterious. But to him that can read the Scriptures without prejudice from Education, *&c.* it will manifeftly appear that the Scripture is full and Intelligible, both as to the Crime and means to detect the culpable. He that fhall hereafter fee any perfon, who to confirm People in a falfe belief, about the power of Witches and Devils, pretending to a fign to confirm it; fuch as knocking off of invifible Chains with the hand, driving away Devils by brufhing, ftriking with a Sword or Stick, to wound a perfon at a great diftance, *&c.* may (according to that head of Mr. *Gauls,* quoted by Mr. *C. M.* and fo often herein before recited, and fo well proved by Scripture) conclude that he has *feen Witchcraft performed.*

[156] If *Baalam* became a Sorcerer by Sacrifizing and Praying to the true God againft his vifible people; Then he that fhall pray that the afflicted (by their *Spectral* Sight) may accufe fome other Perfon (whereby their reputations and lives may be indangered) fuch will juftly deferve the Name of a *Sorcerer.* If any Perfon pretends to know more than can be known by humane means, and profeffeth at the fame time that they have it from the *Black-Man, i. e. the Devil,* and fhall from hence give Teftimony againft the Lives of

others, they are manifeſtly ſuch as have a familiar
Spirit; and if any, knowing them to have their
Information from the *Black-man,* ſhall be inqui-
ſitive of them for their Teſtimony againſt others,
they therein are dealing with ſuch as have a *Fa-
miliar-Spirit.*

And if theſe ſhall pretend to *ſee the dead* by
their *Spectral Sight,* and others shall be inquiſi-
tive of them, and receive their Anſwers what it
is the *dead ſay,* and who it is they accuſe, both
the one and the other are by Scripture *Guilty of
Necromancy.*

Theſe are all of them crimes as eaſily proved as
any whatſoever, and that by ſuch proof as the Law
of God requires, ſo that it is *no Unintelligible Law.*

But if the Iniquity of the times be ſuch that
theſe Criminals not only Eſcape Indemnified, but
are Incouraged in their wickedneſs, and made uſe
of to take away the Lives of others, this is worſe
than a making the Law of God *Vain,* it being a
rendring of it *dangerous,* againſt the Lives of Innocents, and without all hopes of better, ſo long
as theſe Bloody Principles remain.

As long as Chriſtians do Eſteem the *Law of
God to be Imperfect,* as not deſcribing that crime
that it requires to be Puniſh'd by Death.

As long as men ſuffer themſelves to be Poiſon'd
in their Education, and be grounded in a *Falſe
Belief by the Books of the Heathen.*

As long as the *Devil* ſhall be believed to have
*a Natural Power, to Act above and againſt a courſe
of Nature.*

As long as the *Witches* ſhall be believed to have a Power to *Commiſſion him.*

As long as the *Devil's Teſtimony,* by the pretended afflicted, ſhall be received as *more valid to Condemn,* than their Plea of *Not Guilty* to acquit.

As long as the *Accuſed* ſhall have their *Lives and Liberties* confirmed and reſtored to them, *upon their Confeſſing themſelves Guilty.*

As long as the *Accuſed* ſhall be forc't to *undergo Hardſhips and Torments* for their not Confeſſing.

As long as *Tets* for the *Devil to Suck* are ſearched for upon the Bodies of the accuſed, as a token of guilt.

As long as the *Lord's Prayer* ſhall be profaned, by being made a Teſt, who are culpable.

As long as *Witchcraft, Sorcery, Familiar Spirits, and Necromancy,* ſhall be improved to diſcover who are *Witches, &c.*

So long it may be expected that innocents will ſuffer as Witches.

So long God will be Daily diſhonoured, And ſo long his Judgments, muſt be expected to be continued.[177]

F I N I S.

[177] Theſe Notes may fittingly be cloſed by another Extract from our amiable Quaker Poet, who ſeems attentively to have examined the Characters of both the *Wonders* and the *More Wonders:*

"In the ſolemn Days of Old,
  Two Men met in Boſton Town—
One a Merchant Frank and bold,

One a Preacher of renown.

Cried the laſt, in bitter Tone—
' Priſoner of the Wells of Truth,
Satan s Hireling thou haſt ſown
  With his Tares the Heart of Youth !'

Spake the honeſt Merchant then—
  God be Judge 'twixt Thee and I ;
All thou knowſt of Truth hath been
  Unto Men like thee a lie."

APPENDIX.

NUMBER I.

Examination of Giles Cory.

WHY this Examination was not given by Dr. Mather, in his Account of the Witchcraft, cannot be certainly ſtated ; while it may be conjectured that it was omitted for one of the two following Reaſons : 1ſt, it may have been thought not ſufficiently damning to the Accuſed ; or, 2dly, it may have been rejected, as a great Part of the Proceedings was, for want of Room. It ſeems not now to be among the Copies of thoſe Proceedings recently made, or Mr. Woodward would not have omitted it in his Work. It is given here, as tranſcribed by Mr. David Pulſifer, for the Edition of the *More Wonders*, &c., publiſhed in Salem by Cuſhing & Appleton, in 1823. The previous Edition, of courſe, does not contain it.[1]

The Examination of Giles Cory, at a Court at Salem Village, held by John Hathorn and Jonathan Curwin, Eſqrs., April 19, 1692.

Giles Cory, you are brought before Authority upon

---

[1] As will be ſeen, Mr. Pulſifer modernized the Orthography, while we have corrected the Punctuation, in a few Inſtances, and capitalized it agreeable to our previous uniform Old Style.

high Sufpicion of fundry Acts of Witchcraft. Now tell us the Truth in this Matter.

I hope, through the Goodnefs of God, I fhall; for that Matter I never had no Hand in, in my Life.

Which of you have feen this Man hurt you?

Mary Wolcott, Mercy Lewis, Ann Putman, Jr., and Abigail Williams affirmed he had hurt them.

Hath he hurt you too? fpeaking to Elizabeth Hubbard. She going to anfwer was prevented by a Fit.

Benjamin Gold, Hath he hurt you?

I have feen him feveral Times, and been hurt after it, but cannot affirm that it was he.

Hath he brought the Book to any of you?

Mary Wolcott and Abigail Williams and others affirmed he had brought the Book to them.

Giles Cory, they accufe you, or your Appearance, of hurting them, and bringing the Book to them. What do you fay? Why do you hurt them? Tell us the Truth.

I never did hurt them.

It is your Appearance hurts them, they charge you; tell us. What have you done?

I have done nothing to damage them.

Have you never entered into Contract with the Devil?

I never did.

What Temptations have you had?

I never had Temptations in my Life.

What! have you done it without Temptations?

What was the Reafon (faid Goodwife Bibber) that you were frighted in the Cow-houfe? And then the Queftionift was fuddenly feized with a violent Fit.

Samuel Braybrook, Goodman Bibber, and his Daughter, teftified that he had told them this Morning that he was frighted in the Cow-houfe.

Cory denied it.

This was not your Appearance but your Perfon, and you told them fo this Morning. Why do you deny it?

What did you fee me in the Cow-houfe?

I never faw nothing but my Cattle.

Divers witneffed that he told them he was frighted. Well, what do you fay to thefe Witneffes?

What was it frighted you?

I do not know that ever I fpoke the Word in my Life.

Tell the Truth. What was it frighted you?

I do not know any Thing that frighted me.

All the Afflicted were feized now with Fits, and troubled with Pinches. Then the Court ordered his Hands to be tied.

What! Is it not enough to act Witchcraft at other Times, but muft you do it now in Face of Authority?

I am a poor Creature and cannot help it.

Upon the Motion of his Head again, they had their Heads and Necks afflicted.

Why do you tell fuch wicked Lies againft Witneffes, that heard you fpeak after this Manner, this very Morning?

I never faw anything but a black Hog.

You faid that you were ftopped once in Prayer; what ftopt you?

I cannot tell. My Wife came towards me and found Fault with me for faying living to God and dying to Sin.

What was it frighted you in the Barn?

I know nothing frighted me there.

Why there are three Witneffes that heard you fay fo to-day.

I do not remember it.

Thomas Gold teftified that he heard him fay, that he knew enough againft his Wife, that would do her Bufinefs.

What was that you knew againft your Wife?

Why, that of living to God, and dying to Sin.

The Marfhal and Bibber's Daughter confirmed the fame; that he faid he could fay that that would do his Wife's Bufinefs.

I 'have faid what I can fay to that.

What was that about your Ox?

I thought he was hipt.

What Ointment was that your Wife had when fhe was feized? You faid it was Ointment fhe made by Major Gidney's Direction.

He denied it, and faid fhe had it of Goody Bibber, or from her Direction.

Goody Bibber faid it is not like that Ointment.

You faid you knew upon your own Knowledge, that fhe had it of Major Gidney.

He denied it.

Did you not fay, when you went to the Ferry with your Wife, you would not go over to Bofton now, for you fhould come yourfelf next Week?

I would not go over becaufe I had not Money.

The Marfhal teftified he faid as before.

One of his Hands was let go, and feveral were afflicted. He held his Head on one Side, and then the Heads of feveral of the Afflicted were held on one Side. He drew in his Cheeks, and the Cheeks of fome of the Afflicted were fuckt in.

John Bibber and his Wife gave in Teftimony concerning fome Temptations he had to make away with himfelf.

How doth this agree with what you faid, that you had no Temptations?

I meant Temptations to Witchcraft.

If you can give way to felf-murther, that will make way to Temptation to Witchcraft.

Note.—There was Witnefs by feveral, that he faid he would make away with himfelf, and charge his Death upon his Son.

Goody Bibber teftified that the faid Cory called faid Bibber's Hufband, Damned Devilifh Rogue.

Other vile Expreffions teftified [to] in open Court by feveral others.

Salem Village, April 19, 1692. Mr. Samuel Paris being defired to take in Writing the Examination of Giles Cory, delivered it in; and upon hearing the fame, and feeing what we did fee at the Time of his Examination, together with the Charge of the afflicted Perfons againft him, we committed him to their Ma- · jefties Gaol.[2]

JOHN HATHORN.

NUMBER II.

THE following Ballad, in the Chevy Chafe Style, was cut from a Newfpaper fixteen years ago. No one at this Day will probably require to be informed who was the Author of it, as but *one* Perfon probably *could* have written it. I have not looked over the Poems of Mr. Whittier to fee if it be there. Any one having an inclination may do fo. The Introduction accompanied it, on its firft appearance:

[2] It does not appear that thefe Minutes of Examination were read to the Accufed; or that any Opportunity was afforded him to correct any Misftatements which the biaffed Scribe might have made, carelefly or purpofely; while, viewing the Cafe as it ftands, it feems incredible that the Accufed could have been thought deferving of even a lenient Reprimand. Too humiliating for Contemplation!

The following Ballad is handed in for Prefervation as illuftrative of that dark Period in our local Hiftory. Giles Corey and his Wife lived in what is now Danvers, and the Spot is now pointed out on the Eftate of Hon. Daniel P. King where their Houfe formerly ftood. The Localities are faft fading out from Remembrance, and I venture the Suggeftion that it may be in the Province of the Hiftorical Department of our Effex Inftitute to mark them by fome permanent Monumental Erection.—*Salem Obferver.*

GILES COREY AND GOODWYFE COREY.

A BALLAD OF 1692.

Come all New-England Men
And hearken unto me,
And I will tell what did befalle
Upon ye Gallows Tree.

In Salem Village was the Place
As I did heare them faye,
And Goodwyfe Corey was her Name
Upon that paynfull Daye:

This Goody Corey was a Witch
The People did believe,
Afflicting of the Godly Ones
Did make them fadlie Greave.

There were two pyous Matron Dames
And goodly Maidens Three,
That cryed upon this heynous Witch
As you fhall quicklie fee.

Goodwyfe Bibber, fhe was one,
And Goodwyfe Goodall two,

Thefe were ye fore afflicted ones
By Fyts and Pynchings too:

And thofe Three Damfels fair
She worried them full fore,
As all could fee upon their Arms
The divers Marks they bore.

And when before the Magiftrates
For Tryall fhe did ftand,
This Wicked Witch did lye to them
While holding up her Hand;

" I pray you all Good Gentlemen
Come liften unto me,
I never harmed thofe two Goodwyfes
Nor yet thefe Children Three:"

" I call upon my Saviour Lord "
(Blafphemoufly fhe fayed)
" As Witnefs of my Innocence
In this my hour of Need."

The Godly Minifters were fhockt
This Witch-prayer for to hear,
And fome did fee ye Black Man* there
A whifpering in her Eare.

The Magiftrates did faye to her
Moft furely thou doth lye,
Confefs thou here thy hellifh Deeds
Or ill Death thou muft dye.

She rent her Cloaths, fhe tore her Haire,
And lowdly fhe did crye,

* Satan.

" May Chrifte forgive mine Enimies
    When I am called to dye."

This Goodwyfe had a Goodman too,
    Giles Corey was his Name,
In Salem Gaol they fhut him in
    With his blafphemous Dame.

Giles Corey was a Wizzard ftrong,
    A ftubborn Wretch was he,
And fitt was he to hang on high
    Upon ye Locuft Tree:

So when before ye Magiftrates
    For tryall he did come,
He would no true Confeffion make
    But was compleatlie dumbe.

" Giles Corey," faid ye Magiftrate,
    " What haft thou heare to pleade
To thefe who now accufe thy foule
    Of Crymes and horrid Deed ?"

Giles Corey—he fayde not a Word,
    No single Word fpake he:
" Giles Corey," fayth ye Magiftrate,
    " We'll prefs it out of thee."

They got them then a *heavy Beam*,
    They layde it on his Breaft,
They loaded it with heavy Stones,
    And hard upon him preft.

" More weight," now fayd this wretched Man,
    " More weight," again he cryed,
And he did no Confeffion make
    But wickedlie he Dyed.

Dame Corey lived but fix Dayes more,
    But fix Day's more lived fhe,
For She was hung at Gallows Hill
    Upon ye Locuft Tree.

Rejoyce all true New-England Men,
    Let Grace ftill more abounde,
Go fearch ye Land with myght and maine
    Till all thefe Imps be founde:

And that will be a glorious Daye,
    A goodlie Sight to fee,
When you fhall hang thefe Brands of Fyre
    Upon ye Gallows Tree.

NUMBER III.

Teftimony of William Beale, of Marble-head, againft Mr. Philip Englifh of Salem, Given Auguft 2d, 1692. Taken from the Original.

AS Philip Englifh was a Man of a large Eftate for thofe Days, and carried on an extenfive Bufi-nefs, it may be thought fingular that Mr. Calef fhould make no Mention of his Cafe in his Work. It may be that he had not fufficient Data for the Purpofe; or, more probably, it may have been, that for certain Reafons he chofe to leave the Matter in the Hands of the two Minifters of the Old South, who, or one of whom, had not the Independence to work openly with Mr. Calef, but who, clandeftinely, took the Part of the Accufed, and helped him to efcape. However this may have been, fo far as Mr. Willard was con-

cerned, enough will have been feen in Mr. Calef's
Work to caufe an Agitation of the Queftion. And
yet, it will appear, from what is to follow, that Mr.
Moody (then with Mr. Willard in the Old South)
was the principal Inftrument in the Protection and
final Efcape of Mr. Englifh and his Wife from the
Jaws of a "blind Ferocity."

The Teftimony of William Beale, which follows
was probably contrived by certain Parties to recover
Property owned or claimed by Mr. Englifh. At the
Time of his Arreft, he owned a Ship of 170 Tons,
named the Porcupine, which was commanded by
Robert Bartel, whofe Son, William Bartel, was living
in 1739, at the Age of 45.

Mr. Englifh, it is faid, was an Epifcopalian. Whether his Sentiments had anything to do with his being
proceeded againft, does not appear. He ftated that
by the Profecution he was damaged £1,500. A Petition of his to the Committee appointed by the General
Court to compenfate Sufferers may be feen in Mr.
Woodward's *Collections*, ii, 233. It is curious to fee
now the Awards made to the Survivors of thofe
whofe Mothers and Fathers had been judicially murdered! A few Pounds feems to have fettled the Account.

What follows, previous to William Beale's Teftimony, although once printed, will be quite new, probably, to the Majority of Readers; and it is due to
the Memory of a perfecuted Family to perpetuate it
in Connection with the wicked Attempt at their Ruin.

About the Year 1810, the Rev. Timothy Alden
was engaged in preparing a Catalogue of Books for
the Maffachufetts Hiftorical Society. While in this
Employment he procured from the Rev. William
Bentley, D.D., of Salem, the enfuing Account of

Mr. Englifh. What led to this Refult was Mr. Alden's Endeavors to obtain Information concerning a Portfmouth Gentleman. Mr. Alden was then much interefted in Portfmouth Affairs. Dr. Bently proceeds: "In the Times of the Witchcraft in Salem Village, no Perfon diftinguifhed for Property, and known in the commercial World, was accufed but Philip Englifh.3 He came young into America, from the Ifland of Jerfey, lived in the Family of Mr. Hollingworth, a rich Inhabitant of Salem, and afterwards married his only Daughter and Child, Sufanna. The Wife had received a better Education than is common even at this Day [1809], as Proofs I hold fufficiently difcover.

"From fome Prejudices, as early as April 21ft, 1692, fhe was accufed of Witchcraft, examined, and committed to Prifon in Salem. Her Firmnefs is memorable. Six Weeks fhe was confined; but, being vifited by a fond Hufband, her Hufband was alfo accufed, and confined in the fame Prifon. By the Interceffion of Friends, and by a Plea that the Prifon was crowded, they were removed to Arnold's Jail in Bofton, till the Time of Trial.

"In Bofton, upon giving Bail, they had the Liberty of the Town, only lodging in Prifon. Upon their Arrival, Meffrs. Willard and Moodey vifited them, and difcovered every Difpofition to confole them in their Diftrefs. On the Day before they were to return to Salem for Trial, Mr. Moodey waited upon them in the Prifon, and invited them to publick Worfhip. On the Occafion he chofe for the Text, IF THEY PERSECUTE YOU IN ONE CITY, FLEE TO ANO-

---

3 This Opinion of the Doctor may be queftioned, fo long as we do not know by what Standard he meafured Wealth at that Time.

THER. In the Difcourfe, with a manly Freedom, he juftified every Attempt to efcape from the Forms of Juftice, when Juftice was violated in them. After Service Mr. Moodey vifited the Prifoners in the Gaol, and afked Mr. Englifh whether he took Notice of his Difcourfe? Mr. Englifh faid he did not know whether he had applied it as he ought, and wifhed fome Converfation upon the Subject. Mr. Moodey then frankly told him that his Life was in Danger, and he ought by all means to provide for an Efcape. Many, faid he, have fuffered. Mr. Englifh then replied, God will not fuffer them to hurt me. Upon this, Mrs. Englifh faid to her Hufband, Do you not think that they, who have fuffered already, are innocent? He faid, Yes. Why then may not we fuffer alfo? Take Mr. Moody's Advice. Mr. Moody then told Mr. Englifh, that, if he would not carry his Wife away, he would. He then informed him, that he had perfuaded feveral worthy Perfons in Bofton, to make Provifion for their Conveyance out of the Colony; and, that a Conveyance had been obtained, encouraged by the Governour, Gaoler, &c., which would come at Midnight, and that proper Recommendations had been obtained to Gov. Fletcher of New-York; fo that he might give himfelf no concern about any one Circumftance of the Journey; that all Things were amply provided. The Governour alfo gave Letters to Gov. Fletcher, and, at the Time appointed, Mr. Englifh, his Wife, and Daughter were taken and conveyed to New York. He found that, before his Arrival, Mr. Moodey had difpatched Letters, and the Governour, with many private Gentlemen came out to meet him; and the Governour entertained him at his own Houfe, and paid him every Attention, while he remained in the City. On the next Year he returned.[4]

"In all this Bufinefs, Mr. Moody openly juftified Mr. Englifh, and, in defiance of all the Prejudices which prevailed, expreffed his Abhorrence of the Meafures which had obliged a ufeful Citizen to flee from the Executioners. Mr. Moodey was commended by all difcerning Men; but he felt the angry Refentment of the deluded Multitude of his own Times; among whom, fome of high Rank were included. He foon after left Bofton and returned to Portfmouth.

"Mrs. Englifh died in 1694, at 42 Years of Age, in Confequence of the ungenerous Treatment fhe had received. Her Hufband died at 84 Years of Age, in 1734.

"This is the Subftance of Communications made to me at different Times from Madam Sufanna Hathorne, his great-grand-Daughter, who died in Salem, 28 Auguft, 1802, at the Age of 80 Years, who received the Account from the Defcendants of Mr. Englifh, who dwelt upon his Obligations to Mr. Moodey with great Pleafure."

William Beale[5] of Marbllee Head, aged upward of Sixty Yeares, teftifieth and faith, that laft March paft was twelve Moenth, towards the latter end of the Moenth; then myfelf beeinge in the Houfe of George

---

[4] Mr. Englifh was arrefted by Jacob Manning, the Deputy Marfhal, 31 May, 1692. Mrs. Englifh was committed on April 22d, preceding. The Time of their Transfer to Bofton, I do not find; but Mr. Englifh was in Prifon about nine Weeks. Hence it is inferred that their Efcape was about the firft of Auguft following. See Felt, *Annals of Salem*, ii, 479.

[5] Of this Perfon, I have not attempted to add anything to what is contained in Lewis's *Lynn* and Savage's *Dictionary*. Perhaps he was wife enough to keep out of the Way of Philip Englifh after his Return.

Bonfeilds, of Marbllee Head, whither I repaired, that
I might haue helpe to nurfe, or Looke after mee, becaufe of a very greate and wracking Paine had feized
upp on my Body, and the Diftemper of the Small Pox
then beeing in my Houfe, and my Son Jamis at the
fame Time then in my Houfe, lying fick; then towards the latter End of that Moenth, Aforefayed, in
that Houfe, as I lay in my Bed, in the Morneinge,
prefently after it was faiere light abroade in the Roome
where I lay in my Bed, which was layed lowe and
neere unto the Fire, towards the norward part of the
Roome; I beeing broade Awake, I then faw upon the
fouth Iaume [Jamb] of that Chimny, A darke Shade
which couered the Iaume of that Chimney aforefayed,
from the under Floore to the upper Flloore, and alfoe
A dar[k]nefs more then it was beefore, in the foutherne
Part of the Houfe, and alfoe in the Middllee of the
Darknefs, in the Shade uppon the Iaume of the Chimny aforefayed, I beeheld fomethinge of the Forme or
Shape of A Man. I tooke moft notice of his Legs, becaufe they weere of A very greate Statute, or Bignefs.
I wondred at the Sighte, and therefore I turned my
Head as I lay in my Bed, and caft my Eyes towards the
fouth Side of the Houfe, to fee if the Sun weere rifen, or
whether there weere any Perfon or anythinge in the
Houfe, which by the help of the Sun might caufe fuch
A Shade or Shape, but I faw non, nor any Lighte of
the Sun in that Room then. I then turned my Head
uppon the Pillow, where it was before, I faw in the
darknefs aforefayed the plaine Shape or els the Perfon
of Phillip Englifh of Salem, the which, Reports fay,
married with William Hollingworths[6] Daughter of

---

[6] Mr. Savage fays that Mr. Hollingworth's Name was *Richard.*
Beale, though apparently much wanting in Senfe, may be fuppofed to
have known the given Name of a
prominent Man like Hollingworth,

Salem, ackcordinge to my beft Iudgement, Knoledg
and Underftandinge of him, as I had formerly Knoledg
and Ackyuaintance with him, my Coniecktures of him
and thcfe Paffages aforefayed were as followeth : what is
this Mans buifnefs heere now ? I remember not that
euer I .bought or fold with him, either more or lefs,
or which way came hee hither, fo foone this Morneinge,
by Land or by Water ; or hath he been at Marbllee
Head all Nighte ? And then laboreing to correckt my
[Thoughts] not to thinke that hee was A Wich, and
flyinge to our Omnipotent Jehouah for his Bleffing
and Protecktion, by fecret Eiaculations, inftantly the
Roome, aforefayed, became cleare, and the Shape,
Shade, or Perfon vanifhed ; and this was about the
Time News was brought to mee in the Morning, that
my Son James was very like to recover of the Small Pox,
which I left at Home fick ; and the fame Day, in the
After noone, came News that hee was fuddenly ftrooke
with A Paine on his Side, and did not expeét to liue
three Houres ; and according to my Iudgment, before
three Houres weere ended, Newes came that he was
departed this Life, at which Docktor Iackfon, which
was his Docktor, and William Dagget, which was his
Nurfe, both of Marbllee Head, told mee that they Ad-
mired and Wondred ; and it was not many Moenths
before, that my Son George Beale, departed this Life in
the fame Houfe, and complained of A ftoping in his
Throate, after he was recouered of the Small Pox.

with whom he was probably well
acquainted. It feems however, that
Beale confounded the Name of the
Son with that of the Father. The
Hollingworth Family came to Sa-
lem in 1635. The Name is of-
ten fince fpelt *Hollingfworth*. See
Founders of N. Eng. P. 40.

Hee deceafed Ianuary the 23 before my Son Eames
deceafe aforefayde.

Marbllee Head   Attefted to this Truth by
Aguft the 2*cond*   mee WILLIAM BEALE.
1692

Far[ther] this Deponent teftifieth that in the Springe
of the Yeare before the New England Forces went for
Cannady, Phillip Englifh aforefayed, came into a
Neighbors Houfe where this Deponent then was prefent, and then in a fawning and flattering Manner,
fayed to me: You are him which can give mee A good
Evidence in fhewing mee the Bounds of my Land.
This Deponent replyed, and fayed, I know not of any
you have; Phillip Englifh replyed yes you doe, and
If you will I[le pay] you well. I have a Peice of
eighte in my Pocket for you, and named A Peice of
Land ly[ing] a certaine Diftance from my Houfe,
which I think Mr. Richard Reede[7] of Marblle [Head]
was then and is now in Poffeffion of it; this Deponent
replyed, doe not tell mee of your Peice of eight, for
If I bee called, I muft give Evidence againft you, and
told him what I muft fay; at which hee feemed to
bee moued, and told me that I lyed, with more Difcourfe aboute [it,] and fo then wee departed. Then the
next [Feb?] enfuing, which was about the Time that
the Forces began to com from Cannady, I then haueing
heard that Phillip Englifh aforefayd, had arrefted Mr.
Reade aforefayde, about the Land aforefayed, I then,
as I thought it my Duty in Concience, ackquainted
Mr. Reeds Son with what I could fay concerninge the
Titllee of the Lande aforefayed, and withall told him of

[7] For fome Account of him, con-   by J. W. Reed, Efq. publifhed
fult the *Hiftory of the Reed Family*,   1861, Page 42.

Witnefs, as namely Thomas Farrar Senr,[8] of Linn; then afterward uppon their Requeft I rode to Lin and at Lin Mill there I found Thomas Farare, aforefayed, and as wee rode alonge Lin Commons there beetwixt the Reuerende Mr. Sheapards Houfe and Mr. Leytons, then beinge in difcourfe aboute the Titllee of the Lande aforefayed, my Nofe gufhed out bleedeinge in a moft extrordinary manner; fo that I bllodyed a Hankerfhiff of an confiderablle biggnefs, and allfoe ran downe uppon my Cloaths and uppon my Horfe Mane. I lighted of my Horf thinking the iodginge [jogging] of my Horfe mighte caufe it; but it kept on, Allthough not alltog[eth]er fo bad, till I came to Mr. Reades at Marbllee head, and it hath not blead as I can remember neuèr fince I was a Boy, exept about that time, nor fince that time, exept by Ackcident that it was hurt.

Thiefe Things that are fet downe laft were before the former Euidence. WILLIAM

Owned the aboue written before the   BEALE
Grand Iury vpon the Oath hee had taken in Covrt
Jen^{ry} 12th, 1692.

        Robert Payne
        Foreman.

NUMBER IV.

ON a firft and curfory Perufal of the Examination of the Indian Woman belonging to Mr. Parris's Family, it was concluded not to Print it, and only refer to it; that is, only refer to the Extract from it

---

[8] In the *N. Eng. Hift. and Gen.* Account of this Individual will be *Reg.* Vol. VI, Page 316, fome found.

contained in the HISTORY AND ANTIQUITIES OF BOS-
TON. But when the Editorial labor upon thefe Volumes was nearly completed, a reperufal of that Examination was made, and the refult determined the
Editor to give it a place in this Appendix. His
opinion of it, and of thofe who procured it of the
fimple Indian, has been exprefled in a previous Page.

The Examination is valuable on feveral accounts,
the Chief of which is the Light it throws on the Commencement of the Delufion. It does not appear that
either Dr. Mather or Mr. Calef ever faw it, or their
Accounts of the Beginning of the Tranfactions would
have been more explicitly ftated. The Original (now
for the first time Printed,[9]) came into the Editor's
Hands fome five and twenty Year's fince. It is more
extenfive than any of the Examinations yet brought
to light. This is accounted for by its being the Firft
of that cruel and fenfelefs Series of illegal Proceedings
which ended in fo much Agony, Diftrefs, Wretched-
nefs and Blood.

This Examination, more, perhaps, than any of the
reft, exhibits the atrocious Method employed by the
Examinant of caufing the poor, ignorant Accufed to
own and acknowledge Things put into their Mouths
by a manner of queftioning as much to be condemned
as Perjury itfelf; inafmuch as it was fure to produce
that Crime. In this Cafe the Examined was taken
from Jail and placed upon the Stand, and was foon fo
confufed that fhe could fcarcely know what to fay;
while it is evident that all of her Anfwers were at firft
true, becaufe direct, ftraightforward, and reafonable.
The Strangenefs of the Queftions and the long Per-

---

[9] A brief and garbled Extract is placed after the "29th of March,
among the Records, not dated, but 169½"!

fiftence of the Queftioners could lead to no other
refult but the confounding of what little Underftanding the Accufed was at beft poffeffed of. Hence this
Record of incoherent Nonfenfe here fubmitted ; and
of the fame tenor was nearly all the Evidence ufed,
which took away the Lives of numbers of innocent
People.

The Examination was before Meffrs. Hathorne and
Corwin. The Former took down the refult, which is
all in his peculiar Chirography. The firft Proceeding
printed in Mr. Woodward's Colle&ion, having relation to the Witchcraft affair, is a Warrant for the
Apprehenfion of Sarah Good, and is dated Feb. 29th,
169½.[10] On the next Day, March 1ft, the Conftable,
George Locker, made Return, that he had brought
the faid "Saragh Good," &c. Whether fhe were prefent at Tituba's Examination, does not appear ; while
the Documents fhow that the Apprehenfion of Sarah
Good, and the Examination of Tituba were on the
fame Day.

Tittube the Indian Woman Examined, March. 1. 169½.

Q. Why doe you hurt thefe poor Children ? What
harme haue thay done unto you ? A. They doe noe
harme to mee. I noe hurt them att all. Q. Why have
you done itt ? A. I haue done nothing. I cant tell
when the Devill works. Q. What, doth the Devill tell
you that he hurts them ? A. Noe. He tells me nothing.
Q. Doe you never fee fomething appeare in fome
Shape ? A. Noe, never fee any thing. Q. What Fa-
miliarity have you with the Devill, or what is itt that

---

[10] The Papers inferted in the
Records previous to this are, of
courfe, out of place, as they are of
a later Date. A Rearrangement,
or Recompilation of the Witchcraft
Papers muft at fometime be made.

you converfe withall ? Tell the Truth, whoe itt is that hurts them ? A. The Devill, for ought I know. Q. What Appearance, or how doth he appeare when he hurts them with what Shape, or what is he like, that hurts them A. Like a Man, I think. Yefterday, I being in the Leantoe Chamber, I faw a Thing like a Man, that tould me fearve him, and I tould him Noe, I would nott doe fuch Thing. She charges Goody Ofburne and Sarah Good, as thofe that hurt them Children, and would have had hir done itt; fhe fayth fhe hath feen foure, two of which fhe knew nott; fhe faw them laft Night, as fhe was wafhing the Roome. They tould me hurt the Children, and would haue had me gone to Bofton. Ther was 5 of them with the Man. They tould me if I would nott goe and hurt them they would doe foe to mee. Att firft I did agree with them, but afterward I tould them I doe foe noe more. Q. Would they have had you hurt the Children the laft Night? A. Yes, butt I was forry, and I fayd I would doe foe noe more, but tould I would Feare God. Q. Butt why did nott you doe foe before? A. Why they tell me I had done foe before, and therefore, I muft goe on. Thefe were the 4 woemen, and the Man, but fhe knew none but Ofburne and Good, only; the other were of Bofton. Q. Att firft beginning with them, what then appeared to you; what was itt like, that gott you to doe itt? A. One like a Man, Juft as I was goeing to fleep, came to me. This was when the Children was firft hurt. He fayd he would kill the Children, and fhe would never be well; and he fayd, If I would nott ferue him he would doe foe to mee. Q. Is that the fame Man that appeared before to you? that appeared the laft Night and tould you this? A. Yes. Q. what other Likeneffes befides a Man hath appeared to you ? A. Sometimes

like a Hogge, fometimes like a great black Dogge,
foure tymes. Q. But what did they fay unto you?
A. They tould me ferve him, and that was a good
way; that was the black Dogge. I tould him I was
afrayd. He tould me he would be worfe then to
me. Q. What did you fay to him then, after that?
A. I anfwer, I will ferve you noe Longer. He tould
me he would doe me hurt then. Q. What other
Creatures have you feen? A. A Bird. Q. What
Bird? A. A little yellow Bird. Q. Where doth
itt keep? A. With the Man whoe hath pretty
Things more befides. Q. What other pretty Things?
A. He hath nott fhowed them unto me, but he faid
he would fhowe them me to morrow, and tould me
if I would ferve him, I fhould have the Bird. Q.
What other Creatures did you fee? A. I faw 2 Catts,
one Red, another Black, as bigge as a little Dogge.
Q. What did thefe Catts doe? A. I dont know. I have
feen them two tymes. Q. What did they Say? A. They
Say, Serve them. Q. When did you fee them? A. I
faw them laft Night. Q. Did they do any hurt to you
or threaten you? A. They did Scratch me. Q.
When? A. After prayer; and Scratched me becaufe
I would not ferve hir. And when they went away I
could nott fee, but thay ftood before the Fire. Q.
What Service doe thay expect from you? A. They
fay more hurt to the Children. Q. How did you pinch
them when you hurt them? A. The other pull mee and
hall me to pinch the Childe, and I am very forry
For itt? Q. Whatt made you hould your Arme when
you were fearched? What had you there? A. I had
nothing. Q. Do nott thofe Catts fuck you? A.
Noe, never yett. I would nott lett them. But they had
almoft thruft me into the Fire. Q. How doe you
hurt thofe that you pinch? Doe you gett thofe Catts,

or other Things to doe itt for you? Tell us, how is
itt done? A. The Man fends the Catts to me, and bids
me pinch them; and I think I went once to Mr.
Griggs's, and have pinched hir this Day in the Morne-
ing. The Man brought Mr. Griggs's Mayd to me,
and made me pinch hir. Q. Did you ever goe with
thefe Woemen? A. They are very ftrong, and pull
me, and make me goe with them. Q. Where did you
goe? A. Up to Mr. Putnams, and make me hurt
the Child. Q. Whoe did make you goe? A. A Man
that is very ftrong, and thefe two woemen, Good, and
Ofburne, but I am forry. Q. How did you goe?
Whatt doe you Ride upon? A. I Ride upon a Stick,
or Poale, and Good, and Ofburne behind me; we Ride
takeing hold of one another; don't know how we goe,
for I faw noe Trees, nor Path, but was prefently there,
when wee were up. Q. How long fince you began to
pinch Mr. Parris's Children? A. I did nott pinch them
att the Firft, but thay made me afterward. Q. Have
you feen Good, and Ofburne Ride upon a Poule? A.
Yes, and have held Faft by mee: I was nott att
Mr. Griggs's but once, butt it may be fend fomething
like mee; neither would I have gone, butt that they tell
me, they will hurt me. Laft Night they Tell me I
muft kill fome body with the Knife. Q. Who were
they that Told you Soe? A. Sarah Good, and Ofburne, and they would have had me killed Thomas Putnam's Child laft Night. The Child alfoe affirmed, that
att the fame Tyme, thay would have had hir Cutt of
hir own Head; for if fhe would nott, they Tould hir
Tittubee would Cutt itt off; and then fhe Complayned
att the fame Time of a Knife Cutting of hir. When
hir Mafter hath afked hir about thefe Things, She
Sayth thay will nott lett hir Tell, but Tell hir if fhe
Tells, hir Head fhall be Cutt off. Q. Who Tells

· you foe? A. The Man, Good, and Ofburnes Wife.
Goody Good Came to hir laft Night, when her Mafter
was att Prayer, and would nott lett hir hear, and fhe
Could nott hear a good whyle. Good hath one of
thofe Birds, the yellow Bird, and would have given
mee itt, but I would not have itt: and in Prayer
Tyme fhe ftoped my Eares and would nott lett me
hear. Q. What fhould you have done with itt. A. Give
itt to the Children, which yellow Bird hath bin feverall Tymes feen by the Children. I faw Sarah Good
have itt on hir Hand, when fhe Came to hir, when
Mr. Parris was att prayer: I faw the Bird fuck Good
betweene the fore Finger and Long Fingcr, upon the
Right Hand. Q. Did you never practife Witchcraft
in your owne Country? A. Noe. Never before now.
Q. Did you fee them doe itt now? A. Yes. To Day; ·
but twas in the Morning. Q. Butt did you fee them doe
itt now, while you are Examininge? A. Noe, I did
nott See them, but I Saw them hurt att other Tymes. I
faw Good have a Catt befide the yellow Bird, which was
with hir. Q. What hath Ofburne gott to goe with hir?
A. Some thing I don't know what itt is. I can't name
itt. I don't know how itt looks. She hath two of
them. One of them hath Wings, and two Leggs, and a
Head like a Woeman. The Children Saw the Same butt
Yefterday, which afterward Turned into a Woeman.
Q. What is the Other Thing that Goody Ofburne hath?
A. A Thing all over hairy; all the Face hayry, and a
long Nofe, and I don't know how to tell how the Face
looks; with Two Leggs, itt goeth uprighte, and is ·
about Two or three Foot high, and goeth upright
like a Man; and laft Night itt Stood before the Fire,
in Mr. Parris's Hall. Q. Whoe was that appeared like
a Wolfe to Hubbard, as fhe was goeing from Proctures?
A. Itt was Sarah Good, and I faw hir fend the Wolfe

to hir. Q. What Cloathes doth the Man appeare unto you in? A. Black Cloaths, fometimes, fometimes Searge Coat of other Couler; a Tall Man with white hayr, I think. Q. What Aparrell doe the Woemen ware? A. I don't know what Couller. Q. What kind of Cloathes hath She? A. A black filk Hood, with a white Silk Hood under itt, with Sopknotts, which Woeman I know not, but have feen hir in Bofton, when I lived there. Q. What Cloathes the little Woman? A. a Searge Coat with a white Cap, as I think. The Children having Fitts at this very Time, She was afked, whoe hurt them? She Anfwers Goody Good; and the Children affirmed the fame; butt Hubbard being taken in an Extreame Fitt; after, fhe was afked, whoe hurt hir? and fhe fayd fhe Could nott tell, butt Sayd they blinded hir, and would not lett hir fee, and after that, was once or twice taken dumb hir felf.

Second Examination. March. 2. 169½.

Q. What Covenant did you make with that Man that came to you? What did he tell you. A. He tell me he God, and I muft beleive him, and ferve him fix Yeares, and he would give me many fine Things. Q. How longe a goue was this? A. About fix Weeks, and a little more; Fryday Night before Abigall was Ill. Q. What did he fay you muft doe more? Did he fay you muft write any Thing? Did he offer you any Paper? A. Yes, the next Time he come to me, and fhowed me fome fine Things; fome Thing like Creatures; a little Bird, fome Thing like green and white. Q. Did you promife him this when he fpake to you? Then what did you anfwer him. A I then Sayd this, I tould him I Could nott beleive him God; I tould him I afk my Maifter, and would have gone up, but he ftopt mee, and would nott lett

me. Q. Whatt did you promifs him? A. The firft
Tyme I beleive him God, and then he was Glad.
Q. What did he fay to you then? What did he
fay you muft doe? A. Then he tell me they muft
meet together. 'Q. When did he fay you muft meet
together? A. He tell me Weddnefday next, att my
mafters Houfe, and then they all meet together, and
thatt Night I faw them all ftand in the Corner, all four
of them, and the Man ftand behind mee, and take hold
of mee, to make mee ftand ftill in the Hall. Q. Whare
was your Mafter then? A. In the other.Roome. Q.
What Time of Night? A. A little before prayer Time.
Q. What did this Man fay to you when he took hold of
you? A. He fay goe into the other Room and fee the
Children, and doe hurt to them, and Pinch them; and
then I went in, and would nott hurt them a good while;
I would nott hurt Betty, I loved Betty, but they hall
me and make me pinch Betty, and the next Abigall,
and then quickly went away altogether a[fter] I had
pinch them. Q. Did you goe into that Room in your
own Perfon, and all the reft? A. Yes, and my Mafter
did nott fee us, for they would nottlett my Mafter fee. Q.
Did you goe with the Company? A. Noe, I ftayd and
the Man ftayd with mee. Q. What did he then to you?
A. He tell me my Mafter goe to Prayer, and he read
in Book, and he afk me what I remember, but don't
you remember any thing? Q. Did he afk you noe
more but the frft Time to ferve him, or the second
time? A. Yes, he afk me againe, and if I ferve him
fix yeares and he Come the Next Time, and fhow mee
a Book. Q. And when would he come then? A. The
next Fyday, and fhowed me a Book in the Day Time,
betimes in the Morning. Q. And what Booke did he
bring, a great or little Booke? A. He did nott fhow itt

Aa3

me, nor would nott, but had itt in his Pockett. Q.
Did he nott make you write your Name? A. Noe,
nott yett, for my Miftris Called me into the other
Roome. Q. Whatt did he fay you muft do in that
Book? A. He fayd, Write, and fett my name to itt.
Q. Did you Write? A. Yes, once I made a Marke
in the Book, and made itt with red like Bloud. Q. Did
he gett itt out of your Body? A. He faid he muft gett
itt out. The Next Time he Come againe he give me a
Pin, tyed in a Stick, to doe itt with, butt he noe lett
me Bloud with itt as yett, butt Intended another
Time, when he came again. Q. Did you fee any
other Marks in his Book? A. Yes, a great many,
fome Marks Red, fome Yellow, he opened his Book,
and a great many Marks in itt. Q. Did he tell you
the Names of them? A. Yes, of two, noe more;
Good, and Ofburne, and he fay they make them
Marks in that Book, and he fhewed them mee. Q.
How many Marks doe you think there was? A.
Nine. Q. Did thay write there Names? A. They made
Marks, Goody Good fayd fhe made hir Mark, but
Goody Ofburne would nott tell; fhe was Crofs to mee.
Q. When did Good tell you fhe fett hir Hand to the
Book? The fame Day I came hither to Prifon? Q.
Did you fee the Man thatt Morning? A. Yes, a
litle in the Morning, and he tell me the Magiftrates
Come up to examine me. Q. What did he fay you
muft fay? A. He tell me, tell nothing, if I did he
would cutt my Head off. Q. Tell us true how many
Woemen doe ufe to come when you Rid abroad?
A. Foure of them, thefe two, Ofburne, and Good,
and thofe two Strangers. Q. You fay that there was
Nine. Did he tell you whoe they were? A. Noe,
he noe lett me fee, but he tell me I fhould fee them
the next Tyme. Q. What Sights did you fee? A.

I fee a Man, a Dogge, a Hogge, and two Catts, a Black and Red; and the ftrange Monfter was Ofburnes, that I mentioed before; this was the Hayry Imp: the Man would give itt to mee, but I would nott have itt. Q. Did he fhow you in the Book which was Ofburns and which was Goods Mark? A. Yes, I fee there Marks. Q. Butt did he tell the Names of the other? A. Noe fir. Q. And what did he fay to you when you made your Mark? A. He fayed Serve mee, and always ferve mee. The Man with the two Woemen Came from Bofton. Q. How many times did you goe to Bofton? A. I was goeing and then Came back againe. I was never att Bofton. Q. Whoe Came back with you againe? A. The Man came back with mee, and the Woemen goe away; I was nott willing to goe. Q. How farr did you goe, to what Towne? A. I never went to any Towne. I fee noe Trees, noe Towne. Q. Did he tell you where the Nine Lived? A. Yes, fome in Bofton, and fome here in this Towne, but he would nott tell mee whoe thay were.

NUMBER V.

The Examination of Mary Clark[11] *of Ha-verhill. Taken before Jno. Hauthorn, Efq. and otheir their Majefties Juftices of the Peace, Auguft 4th, 1692.*

THE Accufed, Mary Clark, being called, it was enquired of Mary Walcot, if ever Clark had afflicted her? She anfwered Yes, that is the very

[11] There was a large Family of *Clarks* early at Haverhill. To what Family this injured Woman be-longed, my Materials do not difclofe.

woman. And, upon Mary Clarks looking upon Walcott. and others of the afflicted, they were struck into Fitts.

The Juftices having ufed feverall Arguments (for the Good of her Soul) to confefs, if fhe knew herfelf guilty. She abfolutely denied. And then the Conftable[12] of Haverhill was called; and being afked of what Fame and Reputation Mary Clark was off? He anfwered they had heard fhe was or had been guilty of fuch Things, but, as to any Thing in Particular, he could not fay. The Juftices afked Mary Walcot if fhe were not miftaken in this Woman? Walcot anfwered, This is the very Woman I faw afflict Timothy Swan,[13] and fhe has afflicted me feveral Times. And after a Fitt fhe was then immediately in, fhe faid fhe faw the above Mary Clark afflict Betty Hubbard, and Ann Putnam.

The faid Mary Clark looking upon Walcott, Hubbard, Putnam, Warrin, they were in Fitts.

Mary Walcott haveing a Pinn runn into her Arme fuddenly, faid that Mary Clark did it.

At the fame Tyme Mary Warrin had a Pinn run into her Throat, under her Chin, which Mr. Noice took out.

Sufanna Sheldon, upon faid Examination, had four Pinns taken out of her Hand; faying that faid Clark put in two of them, and Mr. Ufher[14] the other two.

---

[12] In 1687, Jofeph Peafely was chofen Conftable, but there is no certainty that he exercifed the Office in 1692. John Ayer, Jr., fhared the Duties. See Chafe, *Hift. Haverhill,* 145.

[13] Like the Clarks, the *Swan* Family was extenfive at Haverhill; but Mr. Chafe did not find a Timothy.

[14] Perhaps Mr. Hezekiah, of Bofton. It may be he to whom Mr. Calef refers in his *Poftfcript.* See Page 154, *original paging.*

Mary Poſt[15] faid fhe faw the faid Clark afflict Timothy Swan.

Richard Carryer, a former Confeſſor faid he beleeved he faw the faid Mary Clark with ſome others and himſelf baptiſed at Newburry Falls.

Betty Hubbard[16] was ſtruck down, by her looking upon her.

It was aſked, if fhe could ſay the Lords Prayer, perfectly.

She erred much.

Ann Putnam faid that faid Clark had afflicted her by pinching, choakeing, and ſtriking her in the Face, and told her, that her Name was Miſtrifs Mary Clark, but that People uſed to call her Goody Clark.

Ann Putnam faid further, that fhe faw the faid Clark ſtabb Timothy Swan with a ſquare ragged Speare, as long as her Hand. And, being aſked why fhe called it a *ragged* Speare, fhe faid becauſe it was ragged like a File.

Mary Poſt faid fhe faw this Mary Clarks Spirit at the Village Witch-meeting, and that fhe did eat and drink there as the reſt did. And further, fhe has ſeen the faid Mary Clark afflict Timothy Swan.

I, underwritten, being appoynted by Authority, to take the within Examination, in Wryting, Doe teſtify upon Oath, taken in Court, that this is a true Coppy of the Subſtance of it, to the beſt of my Knowledge.

[*All of the Above is in the Hand of Edward Rawſon. There is no Signature attached.*]

---

[15] I do not find the Name of Poſt in Mr. Chaſe's *Haverhill.* There was a Family at Woburn; and, according to Mr. Savage, John Poſt, of that Town, had by Wife Mary Tyler, a Daughter Mary, born 1664, who may have been this Witnefs.

[16] The fame who has been ſo often mentioned as Elizabeth Hubbard. In the next Article of this Appendix fhe is particularly noticed.

NUMBER VI.

An Account of the Life and Character of the Rev. Samuel Parris, of Salem Village, and of his Connection with the Witchcraft Delusion of 1692.

BY SAMUEL P. FOWLER, ESQUIRE.[17]

MR. Parris, whofe Hiftory is fo intimately connected with the Salem Witchcraft Delufion of 1692, was a Son of Thomas Parris of London, and was born in 1653. He was a Member of Harvard College, but did not graduate at that Inftitution. He was at firft a Merchant in Bofton, but not fucceeding in Bufinefs he left it, and offered himfelf as a Candidate for the Miniftry.

The People at Salem Village being without a Paftor, on the 15th of November, 1688, fent a Committee, confifting of three Perfons, viz: Captain John Putnam, Mr. Jofhua Rea, Sen., and Francis Nurfe, "to treat with Mr. Parris about taking minifterial Office." Nothing was done however at this Meeting towards effecting a Settlement, and on the 25th of November, after the Services in the Afternoon, the Audience was ftayed, and by a general Vote, requefted Mr. Parris to take Office. On the 10th of December, 1688, the Brethren of the Church, fent Lieut. Nath'l Putnam, Sergeant Fuller, Mr. Jofhua Rea, Sen., and Sergeant Ingerfoll, who came, they faid, " as Meffengers to

[17] Mr. Fowler has very kindly placed this highly valuable Article at the Editor's Difpofal. It was originally read before the *Effex Inft't.*

know whether Mr. Parris would accept of Office."
He replied, "yᵉ Work was weighty, they fhould
know in due Time." After this, feveral came on like
Errands, but as yet, no Propofals of Maintenance
were tendered.

On the 29th of April, 1689, Deacons Nath'l Ingerfoll and Edward Putnam, Daniel Rea, Thomas Fuller,
Jr., and John Tarbell, came to Mr. Parris, from the
meeting Houfe, where there had been a general Meeting of the Inhabitants, and faid, "being the aged
Men had had the Matter of Mr. Parris's Settlement
fo long in Hand, and effected nothing, they were defirous to try what the Younger could do." Upon Mr.
Parris's afking them what their Will was, they anfwered "they were fent, by yᵉ People to defire him to
take Office, and had concluded to offer him fixty
Pounds for his Salary." Twenty Pounds of which,
was to be in Money, and the Remainder as follows:
Wheat at 4 Shillings per Bufhel, Indian Corn at 2
Shillings per Bufhel, Barley, Rye and Malt at 3 Shillings per Bufhel, Pork at 2 Pence per. Pound, Beef
at 1½ Pence per. Pound.

The Committee being defirous of a fpeedy Anfwer,
Mr. Parris informed them, that he would accept of
their Propofals, provided they would comply with the
following Provifions for his Maintenance: 1ft, "When
Money fhall be more plenteous, the Money Part to
be paid me, fhall accordingly be increafed. 2d, Tho'
Corn or like Provifions fhould arife to a higher Price
than you have fet, yet for my own Family Ufe, I
fnall have what is needful, at ye Price now ftated;
and fo if it fall lower. 3d, The whole fixty Pounds
to be only from our Inhabitants, that are dwelling in
our Bounds, or proportionable to what Lands they
have, within yᵉ fame. 4th, No Provifion to be

brought in, without juft afking whether needed, and myfelf to make choice of what, unlefs ye Perfon is unable to pay in any Sort but one. 5th, Fire Wood to be given in yearly freely. 6th, Two Men to be chofen yearly to fee that due Payments be made. 7th, Contributions each Sabbath in Papers, and only fuch as are in Papers, and dwelling within in our Bounds, to be accounted as Part of the fixty Pounds. 8th, As God fhall pleafe to blefs ye Place, fo as to be able to rife higher, than ye faid fixty Pounds, that then a proportionable Increafe be made. If God fhall pleafe for our Sins to diminifh the Subftance of faid Place, I will endeavour accordingly to bear fuch Loffes, by proportionable Abatements of fuch as fhall reafonably defire it."

Thefe Propofals of Mr. Parris to the Committee were read to them and accepted, and they expreffed their Belief, that the Inhabitants would approve of them. But it would feem that at a Meeting of the People of the Village, May 17th, 1689, Mr. Parris was fent for, when Objections were made againft the 5th and 7th Provifions of his Settlement. "Touching the 5th it was objected, they had no Commons, and therefore could not conveniently give in Fire Wood, becaufe fome muft bring in half Cord, others more, others lefs, &c. Therefore they would allow fix Pounds per annum, one third Money, which would buy 30 Cords, as they had dealt by former Minifters. Parris replied, he was willing to eafe them, but then he defired, that one of them would take the fix Pounds annually, and furnifh him with 30 Cords of Wood, to which Propofal he found none of them willing to confent. He then told them, if he did accept the fix Pounds, it might in Time be infufficient to purchafe 30 Cords of Wood. In reply to the Fears of Parris in regard to the Rife of the Price of Wood, he fays, I had a general Anfwer from many that at four Shillings per Cord, I fhould be fupplied during my Life among them. He continues, after much urging, I replied I would try them for one Year. Mr. Parris fays: "touching his 7th Provifion, nothing at the Time was faid or objected againft Contributions by Papers, for it had been their former ufual Way, but only againft thofe, that dwelled within their Bounds, they urging that fome did not live within their Bounds, yet they were conftant Hearers, and therefore it was meet to have their Help.

"In fine, after much Agitation here, it was agreed on my Part and theirs, that fuch out Perfons had Liberty to pleafe themfelves, in paying to the Minifter or the meeting Houfe. And fo I left them, fully acquiefcing with my aforefaid Conditions, not doubting but that they had truly entered it on the Records, as I took for granted, nor heard any Thing otherwife, till after my Ordination a good while, in another public Meeting of the Village; when another Vote, recorded and read, vaftly different from the Agreement, as above faid—which I then openly did, and ftill muft deny, to be any Contract of mine."

We have now prefented Mr. Parris's Account, of the Tranfactions between himfelf and the People of Salem Village, in regard to his Settlement. This was drawn up by him, and ufed upon his Trial before the Court of Common Pleas at Ipfwich in 1696-7. We have been thus particular in Relation to the Settlement of Mr. Parris at Salem Village, it being one of the Caufes, which led to the moft bitter parochial Quarrel, that ever exifted in New-England, and in the Opinion of fome Perfons, was the chief or primary Caufe of that world-wide famous Delufion, the Salem Witchcraft.

Bb3

Salem Village, fince embraced in the Parifh of Rev.
Dr. Milton P. Braman, in Danvers, Maffachufetts,
was, on the 19th of November, 1689 (when the Rev.
Samuel Parris entered upon his Duties there as a
Paftor and Teacher,) a fmall Hamlet or Village, in-
habited principally by Farmers, but embracing within
its Limits, much adjoining Territory, extending its
Lines to Wills Hill, now Middleton, there being
many Families who attended Worfhip at Salem Village. The number of rateable Polls in the Parifh
was 100. It appears, from the Records, that Mr.
Parris prefented to his Church, upon his Settlement,
a new Covenant and Form of Admiffion for its
Members, together with the Queftion, who were the
proper Subjects of Baptifm? Thefe caufed fome Debate in the Church, but none oppofed the final Action
upon them. Some fingular and unufual Cafes of
Difcipline came before them, but they appeared to
have been difpofed of peaceably. It was not until
the 8th of October, 1691, that we difcover any un-
friendly feeling, exifting between Mr. Parris and his
People. It was on that Day, he fays in his Church
Records,—" Being my Lecture Day after public Service was ended, I was fo bare of Fire Wood, that I
was forced publicly to defire the Inhabitants to take
Care that I might be provided for, telling them, had
it not been for Mr. Corwin (who had brought Wood,
being here at my Houfe), I fhould hardly have had
any to burn." Upon the Paftor's informing the
Church of his Deftitution of Fire Wood, the Brethren raifed a Committee, who were inftructed to fee
the Town Committee, and defire them to make a
Rate for the Minifter. The Committee on Rates
met November 10th, 1691, and reported that they
did not fee good Caufe to take Notice of the Church

Committee, without they had a Letter to fhow, under the Church and Paftor's Hand. Upon this, Mr. Parris complained of the Treatment of the Committee towards him, but more efpecially the Church, whom he faid manifefted an indifference in this Affair. The Committee, whofe Bufinefs it was to raife a Tax to procure the Paftor's Wood, 'ftill continuing to refufe to do it, on the 27th of December, 1691, a Petition was fent to the Quarter Seffions, wherein the Petitioners complain, that "no Reparations of the Village Meeting Houfe has been for a great while regarded, fo that broken Windows, ftopt up fome of them by Boards or otherwife, and others wide open, and is fometimes fo dark, that it is almoft *unufeful*." The Court, upon this Petition, appointed a Meeting of the Inhabitants of the Village, to choofe a new Committee to meet on the 25th of January, 1692, for the Purpofe of affeffing Rates to repair the meeting Houfe, and procure the Paftor's Wood. The Inhabitants of the Village met on that Day, and made choice of Jofeph Pope, Jofeph Holten, Jr., John Tarbell, Thomas Prefton, and James Smith, as their Committee.

This is the laft we hear about this Affair of procuring Wood, &c., probably all further Confideration of it was abforbed in the great Witchcraft Delufion, which was now clofe at Hand, and about to break forth.

We are now brought to the Period of the Commencement of Salem Witchcraft, as it firft developed itfelf in the Family of Samuel Parris, Minifter at Salem Village in 1692.

Mr. Parris's Houfehold confifted, at this Time, of himfelf and Wife, his age being 39 Years, that of his Wife 44 Years, a Daughter Elizabeth, aged nine

Years, a Niece of eleven Years by the Name of Abigail Williams, and two Servants named John Indian, and Tituba his Wife, both Natives of South America, then called New Spain. Thefe were held as Slaves, and Parris probably came into poffeffion of them in fome of his Commercial Tranfactions. By fome Perfons, thefe Indians have been fuppofed to belong to the Aborigines of our Country and to have obtained their knowledge of Witchcraft from the Indian Powows; but this appears to have been a miftake. Mr. Parris's neareft Neighbors were Capt. Jona. Walcut, who had a Daughter called Mary, 17 years of Age, and his Parifh Clerk. Thomas Putnam, who had a Daughter named Ann, aged 12 Years, and a fervant Girl, living with him, named Mercey Lewis aged 17 Years, Mary Warren, aged 20 Years, lived with John Proctor, Elizabeth Booth, aged 18 Years, lived near to John Proctor, Sarah Churchill, aged 20 Years, lived in the Family of Geo. Jacobs, Sen., Sufannah Sheldon, aged 18 Years, lived in the Village. Thefe Girls, together with Abigail Williams, a Niece of Mr. Parris, aged 11 Years, were in the Habit of meeting in a Circle in the Village, to practice Palmiftry, Fortune Telling, &c. It appears by Evidence, given at the Courts, that fome of their Parents and Guardians did not approve of thefe Meetings. Mary Warren, one of the moft Violent of the accufing Girls, lived as we have before faid, with John Proctor, and at laft became his principal Accufer, upon his examination for Witchcraft. Proctor, out of all Patience with the Meetings of the Girls, compofing this Circle, one Day faid he "was a going to the Village to bring Mary Warren, the Jade, Home; for, if let alone, thefe Girls would make us all *Devils and Witches together quickley*. They fhould rather be had to the Whipping Poft; but he would fetch his Jade Home, and thrash the Devil out of her." Proctor said, when Mary Warren was first taken with Fits, he kept her close to the Wheel, and threatened to thrash her, and then she had no more Fits; but the next Day, he being gone from Home, she had her Fits again. If the accusing Girls had been dealt with as John Proctor would have had them, we probably should have had a short Story to tell, about Salem Witchcraft. It is at the Meeting of this Circle of eight Girls, for the purpose of practising Palmstry and Fortune Telling, that we discover the Germ, or the first Origin of the Delusion. We have endeavored to follow them after the Excitement had subsided, for the Purpose of ascertaining their Character in after Life. One only of this Circle, Ann Putnam, confessed her Folly, and sought Forgiveness. Some of them grew up Licentious in their Habits, and all of them appear to have sought Obscurity. Their whole Course, as seen in their Depositions, disclofes much Malignancy, and their Ignorance was so great, that of the Eight accusing Girls, Six of them signed their Names with a Cross. ☓

It was in the latter End of February, 1692, that the Daughter of Mr. Parris, named Elizabeth, aged 9 Years, together with his Niece, Abigail Williams, aged 12 Years, were taken Sick and received such attention from Mrs. Parris as their Case seemed to require. But growing worse under her Treatment, and not being able to ascertain what their Disease was, application was made to their Family Physician, Dr. Gregg, living in the Village. He visited them, and observed that they were afflicted with a sad Distemper, the Name of which he could not tell. Other Physicians were called in, in Consultation, when one of them gave it as his Opinion, that the Children were under an evil Hand. It is probable that it was Dr. Gregg that suppofed the Girls bewitched, for he had exprefled the fame Opinion of many of his Patients when he could not underftand their Difeafe, many times before. It is highly probable that the Opinion of thefe Phyficians went far to form the Belief of not only Parris, but alfo of his minifterial Friends, in the Exiftence of Witchcraft in the Village. Mr. Parris appears to have been much aftonifhed, when the Phyficians informed him, that his Daughter and Niece were, no doubt, under an evil Hand. There is Evidence that Mr. Parris endeavored to keep the Opinion of the Phyficians a Secret, at leaft, till he could determine what Courfe to purfue. At this Time, Mary Sibley, a Member of his Church, gave directions to John Indian how to find out, who bewitched Betfy Parris and Nabby Williams. This was done without the Knowledge of Parris. The Means ufed to make this Difcovery, was to make a Cake of Rye Meal, with the Urine of the Children, and Bake it in the Afhes, and give it to a Dog to eat. Similar difgufting Practices appear to have been ufed to difcover and kill Witches, during the whole Period of the Delufion.

On the 27th of March, 1692, Mr. Parris called together his Church, when he prefented Teftimony againft the Error of fifter Mary Sibley, in giving direction to John Indian in an unwarrantable Way, to find out Witches. Upon Mary Sibley's manifefting Sorrow and Grief for her Conduct, the Brethren of the Church received Satisfaction. By the diabolical Means thus ufed by Mary Sibley, Mr. Parris fuppofed the Devil had been raifed, and feeing the apparent diftreffed Condition of his Family, and not knowing what Courfe to purfue, requefted fome worthy Gentlemen of

Salem, and fome neighboring Minifters to confult to-gether at his Houfe; who when they came, and had inquired diligently into the Sufferings of the Afflicted, concluded they were Preternatural, and feared the Hand of Satan was in them. The Advice given to Parris by them was, that he fhould fit ftill and wait upon the Providence of God, to fee what Time might difcover; and to be much in Prayer for the Difcovery of what was yet fecret. They alfo examined Tituba, who confeffed the making a Cake, and faid her Mif-trefs in her own Country was a Witch, and had taught her fome Means to be ufed for the Difcovery of a Witch, and for the Prevention of being bewitched, &c. But faid fhe herfelf, was not a Witch. Soon after this, there were two or three private Fafts at Parris's Houfe, one of which was kept by the neigh-boring Minifters, and another in Public at the Village. And one general Faft, by Order of the General Court, obferved throughout the Colony, to feek the Lord, that he would rebuke Satan, and be a Light unto his People in this Day of Darknefs.

It is evident from the Account given by Rev. John Hale, who was an Eye Witnefs to many of the Tranfactions at Salem Village, and one of the Minif-ters called for Confultation, that Mr. Parris proceeded with Caution at the Commencement of the Troubles, and was anxious to feek Council and Advice. He likewife wifhed to inform himfelf on the Subject of Witchcraft, and for that Purpofe received as a Loan from Dea. Robert Sanderfon, of Bofton, a Copy of Perkins' Works, which treated upon that Subject.

We are among thofe who believe Mr. Parris was honeft in his Belief in Witchcraft, and that he was not moved in this Affair by perfonal Malice, or the Defire to promote the Caufe of Religion in his Parifh, as has been fuppofed by the Author of the Hiftory of Danvers. We have not as yet, found a Particle of Evidence, that he entertained ill Will againft thofe who were accufed and executed.

Mr. Parris, in common with his minifterial Brethren, appears to have come, after the Confeffion of Tituba, to the full Conclufion, that Witchcraft had broken out in his Parifh, and that the Devil had commenced his Operations in his own Family; and as a faithful Paftor, he fhould not hefitate, for a Moment, to grapple with the Enemy.

It was in this Point of View, that we difcover the Courage of the People of Salem Village, who were engaged in oppofing what they confidered the Machinations of the Devil—they fuppofing that he was the Caufe, operating through the Agency of Witches, of all the Torture and Mifery they beheld, and that, by their Oppofition, they were liable alfo to fuffer from his Malignancy. They believed, alfo, that the Devil was about to eftablifh an Agency, or Kingdom in New England; and had actually commenced Operations in Salem Village. This, Cotton Mather, Parris, and others, were determined fhould not be done, at leaft if they could help it. There was fome very fingular Evidence given at the Courts on this Point. Ann Fofter, of Andover, a confeffing Witch, teftified at her Examination, July 21, 1692, "that fhe was at a Witch Meeting at the Village, where there was a large Number of Witches prefent, and that the principal Difcourfe at this Gathering, was in regard to the fetting up of the Devil's Kingdom at the Village, and making it their Rendezvous!" And another confeffing Witch teftified, at a fubfequent Meeting, that they had, by an unanimous Vote, concluded to fet up the Devil's Kingdom at Salem Village—it being thought, all Things confidered, the moft fuitable Place to begin the Enterprife, and, by fo doing, they were in Hopes it would fpread over New England. This was folemnly and religioufly believed by many, and it required Courage and Pluck to ftand up and refift the Defigns of a powerful, malicious Being, capable, as they fuppofed, of tormenting them in various Ways, deftroying their Cattle, &c.

Parris appears to have been very defirous of preventing his Daughter, Elizabeth, from participating in the Excitement at the Village. She was fent by her Father, at the Commencement of the Delufion, to refide at Salem with Capt. Stephen Scwall. While there, the Captain and his Wife were much difcouraged in effecting a Cure, as fhe continued to have fore Fits. Elizabeth faid that the great *black Man*, came to her, and told her, if fhe would be ruled by him, fhe fhould have whatfoever fhe defired, and go to a *Golden City*. She related this to Mrs. Sewall, who immediately told the Child it was the Devil, and he was a Liar, and bid her tell him fo if he came to her again ; which fhe did accordingly the next Time the black Man came to her. The Devil, it would feem, unaccuftomed, in thofe Days, to experience fuch Refiftance, and utterly aftonifhed at the cool Impudence of Betfy Parris, never troubled her afterwards ; and,—although this Girl was one of the firft Originators of the Witchcraft Delufion, in connection with her Coufin Abigail Williams,—fhe appears to have had, afterwards, but little to do with Witchcraft. This arofe in Confequence of following the fage Advice of Mrs. Sewall, in getting rid of the Devil ; or, what was more probable, in her Father taking her from the weekly Circle of accufing

Cc3

and bewitching Girls, and placing her in a very refpect-
able Family in Salem.

It has been faid that Parris had a Rival in Rev.
George Burroughs, who had Friends in Salem Village,
defirous of his Settlement ; and that that was a fufficient Reafon why Parris fhould appear at the Courts
againft him. We have never feen any Proof of this
Rivalfhip between thefe Clergymen. It is difficult now
to afcertain the Caufe of the Arreft of Burroughs who
was preaching at Wells, at the Time, in his Pulpit.
The Girl who accufed him of bewitching her, was
Mercy Lewis, who was then living with Thomas
Putnam. She formerly lived with Burroughs, when
he preached at the Village ; and, upon one or more
Occafions, he whipped her feverely. This we fufpect
was the true Caufe of her crying out againft him.

It had been faid that Rebecca Nurfe was an Object
of fpecial Hatred to Parris ; but this we have failed to
difcover. We cannot imagine the Caufe of the alleged Complaint of Witchcraft againft Rebecca Nurfe.
She appears to have been an amiable and exemplary
Woman, and well educated for the Times in which
fhe lived. We fufpect, from an Examination of the
Charges brought againft her at the Courts, that fhe had
feveral Times feverely rebuked the accufing Girls for
their Folly and Wickednefs, when meeting in their Cir-
cles. In this Way, fhe probably incurred the Dif-
pleafure of Ann Putnam and her Mother—her principal Accufers. Mr. Parris has often been accufed
of being over Officious, and a fwift Witnefs againft
the Accufed at the Courts. Parris could not be faid to
have been a chief Witnefs in the Profecutions, although
he may be faid to have been a frequent corroborating
Witnefs with his Neighbors. The chief Witneffes
were the accufing Girls, as they were called. At the

preliminary Examinations before the Magiftrates, Parris and others were required to be prefent when the Depofitions were taken down, as related by the Girls, and afterwards made ufe of at the Trials before the Courts.

Thefe being given in and related by Children, and young Perfons, the Court required an Endorfement from fome older Perfons, who witneffed their fuppofed Afflictions, and could atteft to their Depofitions. It is in this Way Mr. Parris's Name, as well as his Neighbors, frequently appear in the Court Documents. Parris appears to have been frequently at the Examinations of thofe accufed of Witchcraft, and put Queftions to thofe on Trial. He alfo acted as a Recorder to the Magiftrates more frequently than others. The Reafon for his being often employed by the Courts was fimply becaufe he was requefted to do fo, and was difcovered to be well qualified for that Purpofe. We have feen the Records of feveral Perfons thus employed, and fhould fay Parris's was the Beft. It was his Practice to take down the Examinations in fhort Hand, — he being a good Stenographer, — and then write them out in full, in a plain, legible Hand.

We have not been able to difcover the Caufe of the alleged Complaint of Witchcraft, againft thofe three excellent Women, viz: Rebecca Nurfe, Mary Eafty, and Sarah Cloyce. They were Sifters, of a good Education, and fair Reputation. It is not to be denied, that the Part Parris took in the Trials of thefe Women, was the chief Caufe of the Oppofition towards him, and led at laft to his Difmiffion from the People at the Village. His principal Oppofers were the Relatives of thefe three unfortunate Sifters. Samuel Nurfe, a Son of Rebecca Nurfe, John Tarbell, who had married her Daughter, and Peter Cloyce, who had married Sarah Cloyce. Thefe three Perfons, together with one Thomas Williams, after the Execution of Rebecca Nurfe and Mary Eafty, and the Imprifon- ment of Sarah Cloyce, became much diffatisfied with Parris, and fought Advice of the Elders in fome of the neighboring Churches, as to the beft Mode of bringing him before a Council to anfwer for his Con- duct in the Witchcraft Delufion. They were Mem- bers of the Village Church, and had for fome Time neglected Public Worfhip on the Sabbath, and abfented themfelves from the Communion. While thefe dif- contented Brethren were confidering what Courfe to purfue againft their Paftor, Parris, either in order to divert their Proceedings from himfelf, or to adminifter Difcipline, on the 14th of Auguft, 1692, caufed the Church to be ftayed, and entered a Complaint againft Samuel Nurfe and Wife, John Tarbell and Wife, and Peter Cloyce, for abfenting themfelves from the Com- munion. This Complaint was entered by the Church, and Brother Nathaniel Putnam, and the two Deacons were chofen to be joined with the Paftor to difcourfe with the Abfentees. Much Time was fpent by this Committee, in endeavoring to obtain Satisfaction from the offending Brethren;—while on the other Hand, they were ftriving by all the Means in their Power, to bring Parris before a Council. At laft, on the 16th of February, 1693, at a Meeting of the Committee of the Church, the Diffenting Brethren gave their Reafons for withdrawing from the Communion.

" Whereas we, Thomas Williams, and John Tar- bell, and Samuel Nurfe, having a long Time gone under the Burden of great Grievances, by Reafon of fome unwarrantable Actings of Mr. Parris, as we efteem them, and were proceeding in an orderly Way, to obtain Satisfaction from him, and had taken fome

Steps thereunto, according to the Advice of fome neighboring Elders. But obftructive to our Proceedings therein, Mr. Parris and fome Brethren of the Church, were appointed by the Church, to demand a Reafon of us, of our withdrawing from Communion. The Regularity of which Proceeding, we do not underftand, becaufe in this Cafe, we efteem ourfelves to be Plaintiffs and Parties offended, and in an orderly Way, feeking Satisfaction, tho' hitherto denied. Our Anfwer to the Church is, that we efteem ourfelves hereby prevented in our Duty, which we account a Grievance, feeing we were firft in Profecution of the Rule of our Lord Jefus Chrift, laid down in Mathew 18 C., 15, 16 vs. Wherefore, if the Church give us the Liberty and Freedom of attending our Duty, as according to Rule bound, poffibly then further Trouble may be prevented, or otherwife, the Cafe will neceffarily and regularly come before them. But if they deny us the Requeft, we fhall, as in Duty bound, give the Reafons of our Proceedings to the Church, or any others, when orderly demanded."

Parris fays, in the Records of the Church, "that thefe difpleafed Brethren were told in Reply to their Communication, that they did ill to reflect on the Church, who, as alfo the Paftor, were ignorant of their Methods, and that they fhould have fpoken with the Paftor himfelf, before they went to confult neighboring Elders. But to this Laft they pleaded Ignorance. So we gave Way to their Requeft of proceeding orderly."

On the 27th of March, 1693, the diffenting Brethren handed to the Paftor the following Document:—

" To our Paftor and Minifter, Mr. Samuel Parris, of Salem Village, and to fome others of the Plantation. We, whofe Names are underwritten, being deeply fenfible, that thofe uncomfortable Differences

that are amongſt us, are very diſhonorable to God, and
a Scandal to Religion, and very uncomfortable to ourſelves, and an ill Example to thoſe, who may come
after us. And by our maintaining and upholding
Differences, that are amongſt us, we do but gratify
the Devil, the great Adverſary to our Souls. For the
Removal of which we have thought meet to proffer
our preſent Thoughts to your ſerious Conſideration,
hoping, that there may be ſuch Methods propounded,
as may be for the ſettling and confirming Peace and
Unity amongſt us, both at the Preſent and for the
Future. And our Deſires are, that ſuch a Foundation may be laid for Peace and Truth, that the Gates
of Hell may not prevail againſt it. And in Order
thereunto, Solomon adviſeth Counſel; and our Deſires are, that a Council of Elders may be choſen, to
hear all our Grievances between Mr. Parris and us,
and determine where the blameable Cauſe is. And
we hope, that their Wiſdom and Prudence may direct
us to ſuch a Method, as may be for our Comfort for
both Preſent and Future."

Much Time was ſpent by the Committee of the
Church, in endeavoring to obtain Satisfaction from
the diſſenting Brethren, while the Latter were ſtriving
by all the Means in their Power, to bring Parris before a Council. At laſt, on the 16th of February,
1693, at a Meeting of the Committee, the diſſenting
Brethren gave their Reaſons for withdrawing from the
Miniſtry at the Village. They are the following.[18]

. After the Paſtor had read the Charges againſt him,
he brought forward his "Meditations for Peace."
This Paper, having been conſidered at the Time as

[18] Being the Same contained in   ted here. See Vol. II, P. 140-3;
Mr. Calef's Part Third, are omit-   or Pages 55-7, original Edition.

an Acknowledgment of his Miftakes in the Witchcraft Delufion, we have given it entire. It is as follows.[19]

Notwithftanding the difcontented Brethren continued to prefs the Acceptance of their Petition, for a mutual Council. Parris refufed to notice it, and fays, "I put it up in my Pocket, and told them I would confider it." It appears, by the Records, that the Acknowledgment of Mr. Parris was firft read before the Church, November, 18, 1694, in the Prefence of the diffenting Brethren, when Tarbell remarked, that if the Paftor had formerly made but *half the Acknowledgment he now had*, it had never come to this. It would feem that the Acknowledgment of the Paftor was not fatisfactory to the Brethren, and they continued to perfift in the calling of a Council. In the Meantime, Parris brought fundry Objections, as he called them, againft Tarbell and his Friends, which were read before the Church, November 13th. Thefe Objections, were as follows:—"Their precipitant, fchifmatical and total withdrawing from the Church; Their bringing forward a factious Libel to the Paftor, confifting of Calumnies, or Reflections on faid Minifter, and others of the Plantation; their impetuous Purfuit of the Minifter at his Houfe, for Anfwer to faid Libel to his great Difquietude; there reftlefs Purfuit of the Minifter, on the 14th of April, 1693, for an Anfwer to faid Libel; their perfifting with great Heat, that their Charge might be read, yea loudly and fiercely before the whole Brotherhood, clamouring againft the Church, and their publifhing under their own Hands, in divers Places of the Country, fundry Obloquies againft the Church; their enfnaring feveral to join them in a Petition to his

[19] See Vol. II, P. 143-8, where this Paper is given entire.

Excellency and General Court, fcandalizing the Church
and Minifter, as unpeaceable with their Neighbors;
their withdrawing their Purfes, as well as their Perfons
from upholding the Lord's Table, and the Miniftry;
their grofs Miftake in their Letter to the Church at
Malden, wherein they profefs fo much Diffatisfaction
with the Doctrine, Practice and Adminiftration of
their Paftor, for above a Year, before the Date of faid
Letter, as that they were forced to withdraw from all
public Worfhip; whereas it is moft notorious, that
they were not wanting as to a Profeffion of much Re-
fpect to their Paftor, all along before, yea, and a confiderable while after the breaking out of the late horrid
Witchcraft." Thefe are fome of the Charges brought
againft the three Brethren by Parris, and he informs
us, "as foon as the public Reading of thefe Articles
was ended, Brother Thomas Wilkins, in a fcoffing
and contemptuous Way, faid openly, 'this is a large
Epiftle.'" It would feem by the Records, that the
diffenting Brethren continued to make ftrenuous Efforts to bring Parris before a Council, which was at
laft recommended by the Paftors of the Churches in
the Neighborhood, when Parris in his laft Attempt to
evade it, propofed to give the difcontented Brethren,
a Difmiffion to fome other orthodox Church, to which
Tarbell replied, "Aye, if we could find a Way to
remove our Living too." After a Delay of more
than two Years, the Church confented to call a Council, who met at the Village, April 3d, 1695. Dr. Increafe Mather was chofen Moderator, and offered the
following Report, which was accepted by the Council,
and prefented to the Church :— 1ft, They unanimoufly
declared that "we judge that altho' in the late and
dark Time of the Confufions, wherein Satan had obtained a more than ordinary Liberty to fift this Plant-

ation, there were fundry unwarrantable and uncomfortable Steps taken, by Mr. Samuel Parris, the Paftor of the Church in Salem Village, then under the hurrying Diftractions of amazing Afflictions; yet the faid Mr. Parris, by the good Hand of God, brought unto a better Senfe of Things, hath fo fully expreffed it, that a Chriftian Charity may, and fhould, receive Satisfaction therewith. 2, They advifed the diffenting Brethren to accept the Satisfaction, which he had tendered in his Chriftian ˙Acknowledgment of the Errors therein committed, and in cafe Mr. Parris finds after all, that he can not with any Comfort and Service, continue in his prefent Station, his Removal from thence, will not expofe him to any hard Character with us. Having obferved that there is, in Salem Village, a Spirit full of Contention and Animofity, too fadly verifying the Blemifh, which hath heretofore lain upon them; and that fome Complaints againft Mr. Parris have been either caufelefs or groundlefs, or unduly aggravated, we do, in the Name and Fear of the Lord, folemnly warn them to confider whether, if they continue to devoure one another, it will not be Bitternefs in the latter End."

The Recommendation of the Council appears to have been fatisfactory to the Friends of Mr. Parris and the Paftor was refolved to continue in the Miniftry. At the fame Time, the Report of the Council was unfatisfactory to thofe Perfons oppofed to Mr. Parris, as it did not recommend his Difmiffion; accordingly, on the 3d Day of May, 1695, a Paper, figned by 16 young Men, 52 Houfeholders and 18 Church Members, was handed to the Rev. Elders, compofing the late Council at the Village, requefting them to give Parris's Cafe a rehearing, and more plainly advife the Paftor to ceafe his Labors, and feek to difpofe himfelf elfewhere, &c. On the 6th of May, 1695, in Anfwer to the Opponents of Mr. Parris, the Council fent a Letter to the Paftor, informing him of the Extent of the Oppofition to his Miniftry, and advifing him to come away from his prefent Station, and unite in calling another Minifter, and forgiving and forgetting all former Grievances.

Mr. Parris appears to have been nettled with the laft Recommendation of the Council for him to leave his Parifh, and fays, in the Church Records, under his own Hand, that the Paper (in Anfwer to the Inftrument and *claffical* Letter from Cambridge) was brought by Deacon Putnam to the Elders, affembled at Bofton, at Mr. Willard's, May 29th, 1695, being the Day of Election after Dinner, when was affembled the Body of Elders, belonging to this Province. This Paper was addreffed to the Rev. Mr. Increafe Mather and others of the Rev. Elders, which lately met at Cambridge, under Date of May 20th, 1695, and figned by 53 Houfeholders and 52 Church members, all belonging to Salem Village. In this Letter, they fay, that the Removing of Mr. Parris from his prefent Station will not unite us in calling another Minifter. That they juftly fear, fhould he be removed, they would be left, as a Sheep, without a Shepherd. Therefore they defire, that Mr. Parris may continue in his prefent Station.

The Council appear to have been at laft fully fatiffied that Mr. Parris fhould leave Salem Village, and they therefore procured a Parifh for him in Suffield, and fent two Meffengers from that Church, to perfuade the Church at Salem Village to difmifs their Paftor. Parris informs us, in his Church Records, that at a Meeting of the Church, held at his Houfe, June 3d, 1695, he acquainted the Brethren, that here were two Meffengers from Suffield, who were looking out for a Minifter, and by the Defire of fome Elders in Bofton, made application to him, and was willing to go with them, if the Brethren pleafed, and in his Abfence for a few Months, they might try if they could (with others who now diffented,) unite in fome other Minifter. But, after feveral Hours debate, both with the Brethren, and fome other Chriftian Neighbors, they all declared an Averfenefs to his Motion. Thereupon thanking them for their profeffed Love to him, he told them, he was not free to go, without their Confent, and feeing they would not let him go, he prayed for them *to keep him, and make much of him.* The fame Day, June 3d, 1695, the Church fent the following decifive Letter to Rev. Increafe and Cotton Mather, faying, "we cannot fault ye Intendment of our Brethren Sergent David Winchell, and Corporal Victory Sikes, Meffengers from Suffield, fent by yourfelves to obtain the Miniftry of our Paftor if we were fo minded, as to part with him. But upon maturing together, this Day both of Church and others, to confult that Affair, do hereby fignify at the Defire of the above Suffield Meffengers, with unanimous Agreement, not one excepted — (fave the Four known Diffenters) we are refolved — *God helping againft fuch a Separation during our ability to prevent it.* And our Paftor tho' otherwife inclined, yet as unwilling to leave fo many of his Flock, as teftify fo ftrong Affections towards him. So earneftly requefting the conftant Helps of your Prayers, and as much otherwife as you can, we reft, worthy and much efteemed Sirs, your needy Brethren.

SAMUEL PARRIS, Paftor,

in the Name of the Church and other Chriftian Neighbors.

To the Rev. Mr. Increafe Mather and }
Mr. Cotton Mather, Jun., Bofton. }

It does not appear that there were any more Efforts made by the Bofton Elders, to bring about a Reconciliation; and it feems that there was always a Majority of the Parifh in Favor of Mr. Parris, remaining with them; and there appears to have been a very general Miftake, with many Authors, in Regard to his Difmiffion from his People, they, fuppofing that he was haftily driven away from the Village. Whereas he continued and maintained himfelf through a minifterial Quarrel of five Years, until he faw fit to difcontinue it, when he informed his Church of his Intentions.

There were three diftinct Matters of Difpute between Parris and his People at Salem Village. The Firft arofe previous to the Breaking out of the Witchcraft Delufion, in Confequence of the Neglect of his Parifh to furnifh him with the ftipulated Supply of 30 Cords of Wood per Annum. The fecond Difpute with the four Diffenting Brethren of the Church, arofe in Confequence of the Courfe purfued by Parris in Regard to Witchcraft. The Third, was in Confequence of his claiming the Parfonage and Lands, under a vote of the Inhabitants of the Village, and their Refufing to pay him his Arrears due him, on his old Lifts of Rates. Thefe three Difputes, caufed a long and continued Quarrel, which at laft attracted the People far and near—was a grave Matter for learned Councils, was brought before the County Courts, and was a Subject for Petition before the great and General Court at Bofton. After it was underftood that Parris was to leave the People at the Village, and that he claimed the Parfonage, a fierce Quarrel arofe between him and the Inhabitants, which was carried before the Court at Ipfwich.

The Matter, without being fettled, was taken from

the Courts, and given to Wait Winthrop, Eliſha Cook, and Samuel Sewall, Eſqrs., and they decided "that Mr. Parris ſhould have ſome of his Arrears paid him, alſo a ſum of Money for his Repairs of the miniſterial Houſe, and be diſmiſſed from Salem Village."

It was during his greateſt Difficulties with his People, that he loſt his Wife by Death. This occurred on the 14th of July, 1696. She was buried in the Wadſworth burial Ground, in Danvers, where can be ſeen a gray Slate Stone,—a fine Specimen of the lapidary Art,—with its Lines as ſharp as on the Day when they were firſt cut, erected over her Grave, on which is the following Inſcription, with thc Initials of Samuel Parris at the Bottom :—

> " Sleep precious Duſt, no ſtranger now to Reſt,
> Thou haſt thy longed wiſh, within Abraham's Breſt—
> Farwell Beſt Wife, Choice Mother, Neighbor, Friend,
> We'll wail the leſs, for hopes of the in the end."   s. p.

After his Diſmiſſion from Salem Village he removed to Concord, Maſſachuſetts, where he lived in 1705; and 1711, preached ſix Months in Dunſtable. He died at Sudbury, February 27th, 1720; Mrs. Dorothy Parris, his ſecond Wife, died there on the 6th of September, 1719. The following are the Children of Mr. Parris :— Elizabeth, who was married to Benj. Barnes, at Concord, January 13th, 1710; Dorothy, married Hopeſtill Brown, of Sudbury, 1718, and died March 4th, 1725; Samuel, who was a Deacon of a Church in Sudbury, died November 22d, 1792, aged 91 Years; Noyes, graduated at Harvard College, 1721, was deranged, and ſupported by the Town; Mary, married Peter Bent, of Sudbury, April 18th, 1727.

[Eleven Years after the Death of Mr. Parris, the following Advertifement appeared. Whether his Defcendants acted upon the Suggeftion contained in it, the Editor is not informed.]

"Any Perfon, who knew Mr. Samuel Parris, formerly of Barbadoes, afterwards of Bofton, in New-England, Merchant, and after that, Minifter at Salem Village, &c., deceaf'd, to be a Son of Thomas Parris, of the Ifland afore faid, Efqr,— who deceafed 1673, or fole Heir by Will to his Eftate in faid Ifland,— are defired to give or fend Notice thereof to the Printer of this Paper; and it fhall be for their Advantage."

[*Bofton News-Letter, No.* 1433, *July* 15*th,* 1731.

NOTE BY THE EDITOR.

WHEN this Edition of the *More Wonders* had paffed through the Prefs, the Publifher brought in the following ERRATA, which, it feems, had been inferted in fome Copies of the original Edition ; and, although feveral of the Errors are quite immaterial, and others have been corrected in the Procefs of Revifion, yet it was thought beft to infert it here entire.

Mr. Woodward informs the Editor, that he copied it from a Copy of Mr. Calef's Work in the Library of the Maffachufetts Hift. Society, which once belonged to Dr. COTTON MATHER, and afterwards to Dr. Jeremy Belknap. Hence it is very probable that this Copy was prefented to Dr. Mather by the Author. However this may have been, the following Extract, written in Dr. Mather's own Hand in the fame Volume, feems odd indeed :

" Job, xxxi, 35, 36. My Defire is, *that* mine Adverfary had written a Book. Surely I would take it upon my Shoulder, and bind it as a Crown to me."

" Co. MATHER."

ERRATA.

[The Reference is to the Pages of the original Edition ; being thofe of the inner Margin of this Edition.]

THE Pages from 48 to 57 may be corrected with the Pen as alfo in the Preface 7 Lines from the End inftead of ufe read me. P. 3. L. 17. f. furioufly r. ferioufly P. 13. L. 2. f. fruitful r. faithful. P. 16 L. 3 from the Bottom f. me r. Mr. P. 18. L. 6. f. drawing r. chaining. P. 28. L. 13. the Word More to be left out. P. 49. L. 12. r. the Ancients did worfhip. P. 52. L. 9. r. the more nearly. P. 55. L. 14. f. unaccountable r. uncomfortable. P. 61. L. 26. after the Word propofe r.

I. That if yourfelves pleafe to take the Trouble with Patience once more to hear the Cafe and give full Liberty of proving, &c. to the Word Place.

P. 63. L. 3. f. proved r. procured P. 65. L. 25. f. dear. r. clear. P. 85. L. 20. r. beft learn. P. 93. L. 12. f. fucking r. fuckling. P. 94. L. 22. r. Mercy Lewis. P. 98. L. 16. Nathaniel Cary. P. 106. L. 31. r. up the Hill. P. 143. L. 8. f. flew r. fled. P. 152 L. 26. f. that he r. he that.

ERRATA, *in the prefent Edition*.—Vol. i, P. 102, Note 114, f. credulous, r. incredulous. P. 110, L. 11, for on r. out. P. 189, N. 174, r. Dr. Felt. Vol. iii, P. 184, L. 1, r. James.

INDEX.

FINIS.

Lightning Source UK Ltd.
Milton Keynes UK
UKHW010059100223
416720UK00001B/246